cupcake sprinkles

P9-BJY-629

a button on a TV remote

---

a chewable vitamin

an eraser

a gum wrapper

_____

a bitcoin

_____

a spy camera

a pigeonhole

a dog tag

Rhode Island (on a map)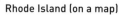

a one-letter word

---

a nail art design

freckles	the eye of a sewing needle

a thimble

a coat button

a pearl onion

the last bite of a cookie

a tooth filling

the date on a penny

a garbanzo bean

an apple stem

a chocolate chip

a snowflake

a cornflake

a robin's egg | a tiger's claw

a spark plug

holes from a bookworm

a worry doll

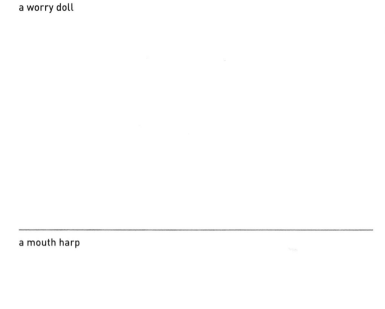

a mouth harp

	sea glass	a yellow polka dot bikini
a chin cleft		a watch chain

a fiber-optic cable

---

small talk

---

spilled salt

a little shop of horrors

a castle made out of ten grains of sand

---

a one-line joke

a first lost tooth

a bit part in a play

a minor celebrity

a stitch in a baseball

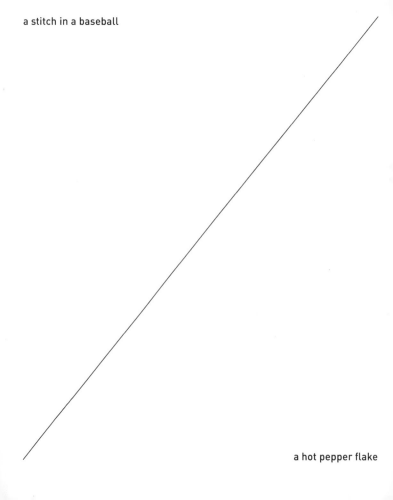

a hot pepper flake

a photo booth picture

the speed of light

---

frilly toothpick

a spitball | an atom

a water droplet | an army ant

an egg stand

a parachutist, from the ground

Pluto

_____

toenail clippings

a flea circus

a plastic thumbtack

small hours of the night

a microcosm

your house, from space

a geometric paperweight

---

a miniature statue of Mount Rushmore

a dollhouse kitchen

---

a mouse on a motorcycle

an eyeglass screw

a window catch

watch gears

a loose thread | a lighter

	a microbe	a typewriter key
an earlobe		a fingerprint

a "vacancy" sign on a roach motel

---

a bar of hotel soap

a lizard's footprint

a ball of lint

a keyhole

a pea in a spoon

a stud earring

baby steps

a laser pointer dot

a mouse hole

a match head

a sunflower seed

a little later

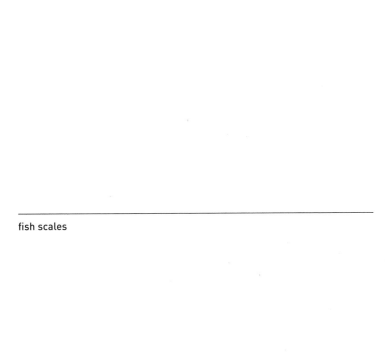

fish scales

the core of a crab apple

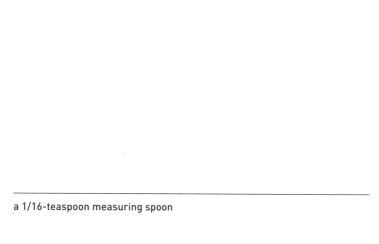

a 1/16-teaspoon measuring spoon

the blink of an eye

a coin slot in a pay phone

an eight-word short story

a hummingbird in flight

the tip of an iceberg

---

a sip of lemonade

---

spots on a banana

a mushroom

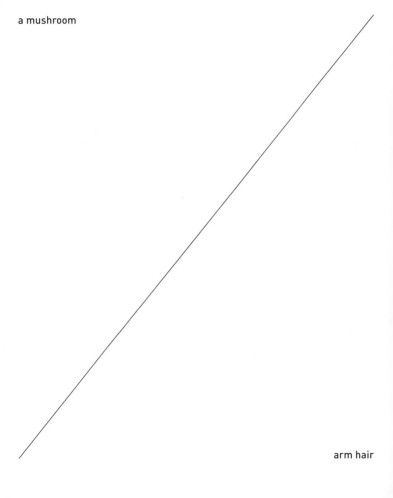

arm hair

a clove

---

a toothbrush head

a fuse

a pinky ring

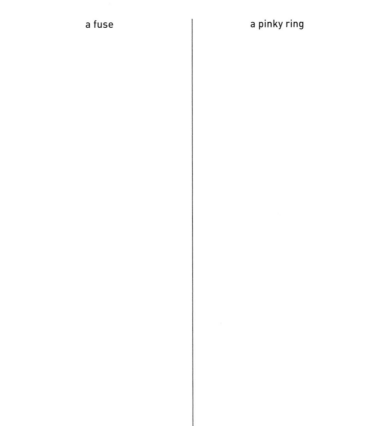

a little brother

bull's-eye on a dartboard

the dot on an *i*   engraving on a wedding ring

a wild strawberry   a dandelion seed

a crawl space

a hermit crab

a blade of grass

tea leaves

small change

a snail shell

a toy soldier

a mini ukulele

a ladybug

a forehead wrinkle

a microchip

a whisper | gold dust

smoke in the distance | a school of minnows

doll shoes

_____

the crest of a wave

_____

a spark

a glass strand on a chandelier

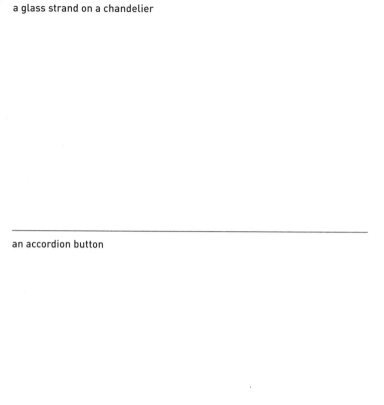

an accordion button

an eyelash

---

pieces of a shattered bottle

a hat for a Christmas elf

a hair curl

a drop of blood

a saxophone mouthpiece

a fishhook

a puzzle piece

---

a lemon drop

a rose petal

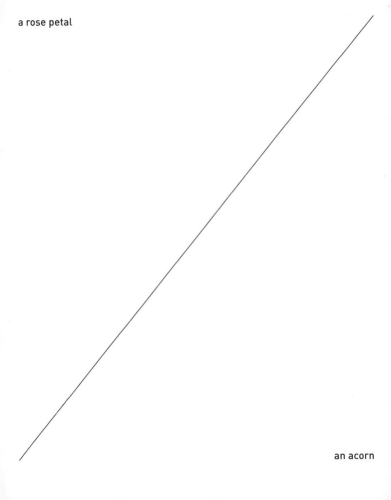

an acorn

a picture locket	a zipper pull
a record player needle	a charm bracelet

a pine needle

---

a marble

---

a grain of rice with "hello" written on it

a birthmark shaped like a heart

a dollop of whipped cream

a BB

pencil shavings

a contact lens

a parrot's eye patch

the head of a worm

a bottle cap

---

a drawer pull

fine print | a pupil

a paperclip bent into the shape of a violin

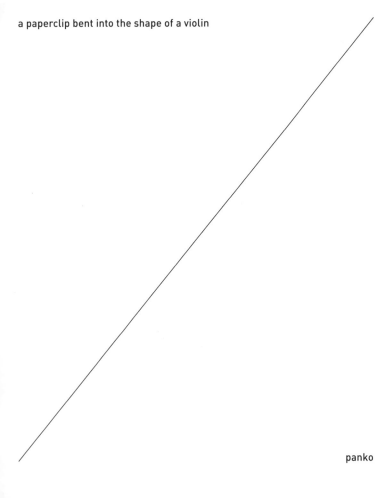

panko

an elbow macaroni

a redwood seedling

a taste bud

a no-see-um

a microdot	glitter
a tea sandwich	popcorn

a window prism

a sugar cube

a paint chip

a pebble

a champagne bubble

a pipsqueak

a cork | wood grain

a shooting star

---

a rolled oat

---

a clothespin

the last ray of sunlight

---

a hole in a pinhole camera

---

a fern frond

a Christmas light

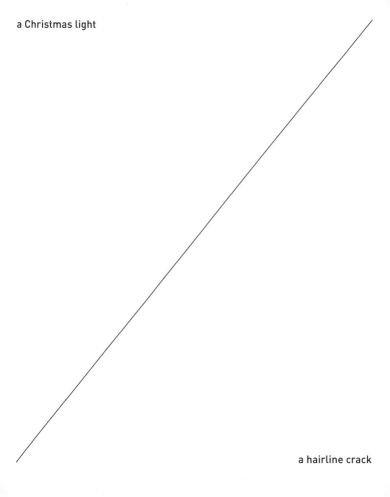

a hairline crack

a portrait on a stamp

---

an airline pack of peanuts

raisins on a bagel

a paper cut

nose hair clippers

---

a dandruff flake

---

a cactus thorn

a barrette

a binder clip

a spot of mold on bread

the head of a cotton swab

a bent staple

an inkwell

a bell on a pet collar

a scar

a vial of poison

a being from the planet Smääll

earbuds

a tilde

a dictionary illustration of a chipmunk

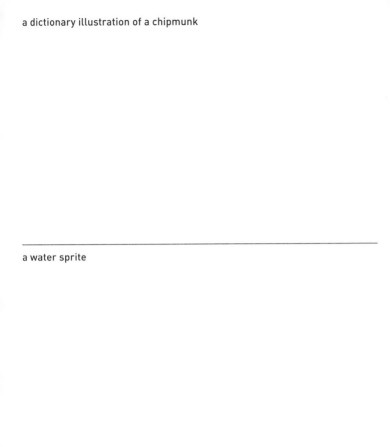

a water sprite

ball bearings

a wart

the high E string on a guitar

a one-word message in a bottle

an amuse-bouche

one "Like" on Facebook

a centimeter mark on a ruler | .0000001 percent

a moth hole in a sweater | a peephole

a retina

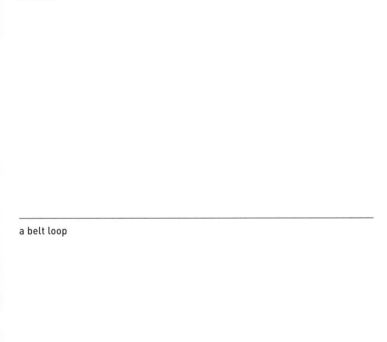

a belt loop

a spring inside a clickable pen

one pixel on a computer screen

a sesame seed

a studio apartment in Manhattan

a shoelace bow

one panel of a comic strip

the first second of January 1

---

a drop of morning dew

the Little Dipper

---

a splinter in a thumb

a sliver of moon

a peanut shell

a matchbox made into a bedroom

something in your eye

a toasted mini marshmallow

_____

one frame of Super 8 film

spiral rings in a notebook

a necklace cameo

the engine of a toy car

a saddle for a sea horse

---

dice for a travel backgammon set

---

a rabbit whisker

a hamster's birthday cake

legroom on an economy class flight

the creases in a bendy straw

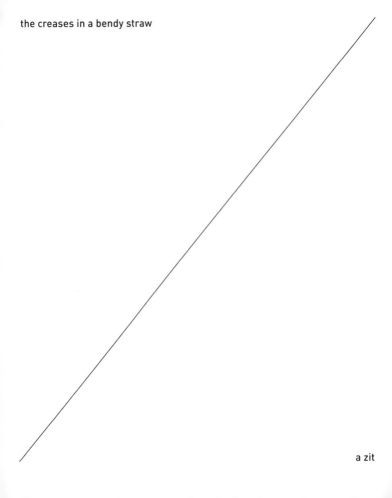

a zit

a chess piece	a short syllable
a window smudge	a half-truth

a doughnut hole

---

the face of a calculator watch

---

a volume knob

the edge of a penknife

a pinprick

mini-blinds

a roly-poly

handcuff keys

---

the letter "K" in braille

---

a T-shirt tag

stained glass

the great seal on a one-dollar bill

a security code on a credit card | the weft of a wool blanket

the spray of an atomizer | an ink stain

a sea monkey

a mocha truffle

---

the shutter speed selector on a camera

a cell in a beehive

a fish egg

a link in a bike chain

a crumble of feta cheese

the space between your toes

a twig in a bird's nest

a carbon atom

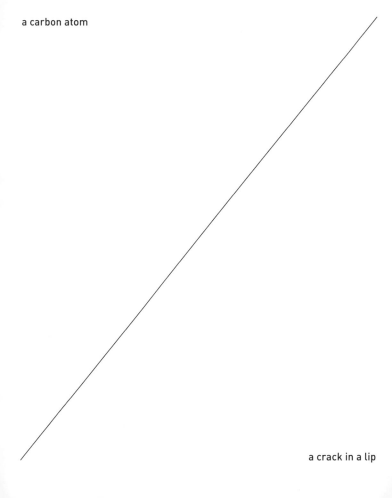

a crack in a lip

crib notes

a logo on a dress shirt

fork tines

a kumquat

---

a slipknot

a ketchup packet

---

a bee's knees

a four-leaf clover | a coffee bean

a parsley sprig on a steak

a dab of wasabi

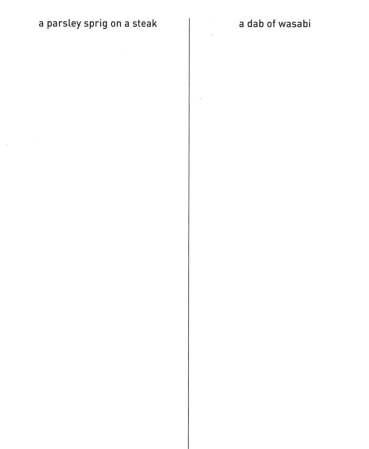

a scarab

a lentil

an icon for an app

an asterisk

a stud on a leather jacket

a tweet

a suction cup

an espresso cup

jewels	a dried currant
a padlock on a diary	a jack

a cherry tomato

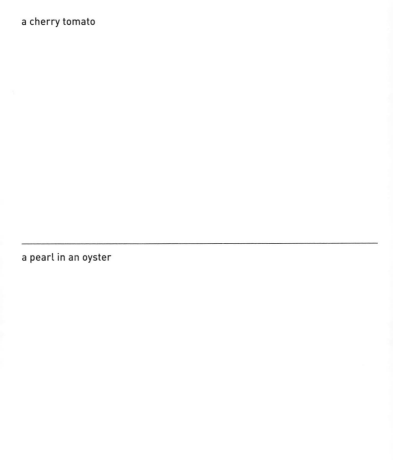

a pearl in an oyster

a firecracker

---

a message on a candy heart

a deflated balloon

a neuron

a roofing nail

a golf tee

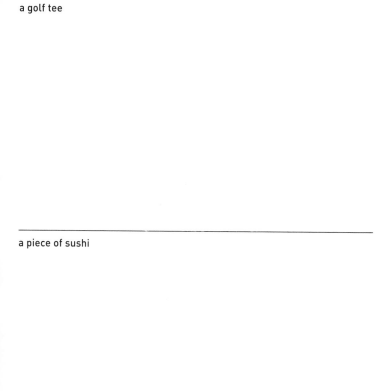

a piece of sushi

a finger puppet

a due date on a library card

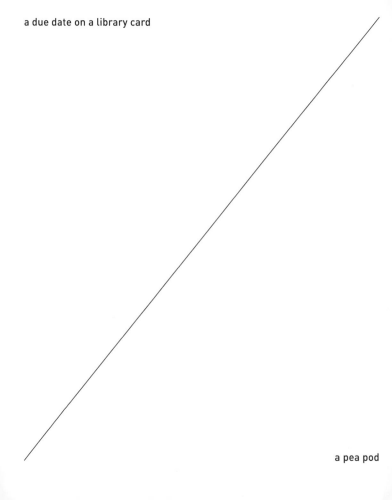

a pea pod

| beard stubble | a rusty screw |

a safety pin

a ticket stub

a butterfly wing

a pixie

a squashed mosquito

a music box ballerina

a number on a rotary phone

a flashlight bulb

a calculator battery

a pomegranate seed

---

a gummy bear

---

a birthday candle

a shoelace hole

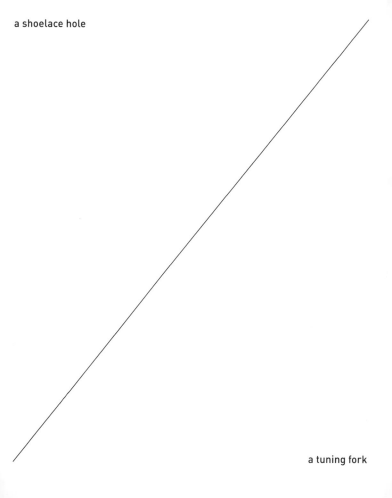

a tuning fork

a sorbet spoon

a spider

a radish top

a petit four

a brooch

a squirrel skull

a pretzel

_____

a spoonful of alphabet soup

_____

goose down

a cherry on top

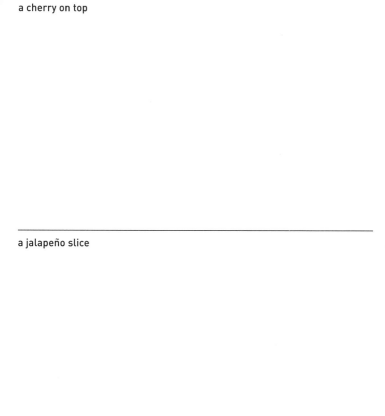

a jalapeño slice

nostrils

_____

the eye of a tiger

a caterpillar

a dash of paprika

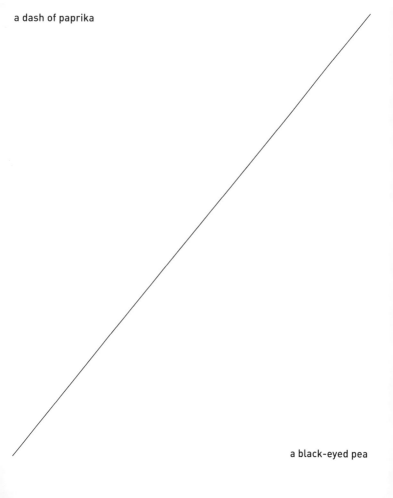

a black-eyed pea

a tuning peg on a mandolin

kittens

a guitar pick

---

a nut and bolt

---

a blood vessel

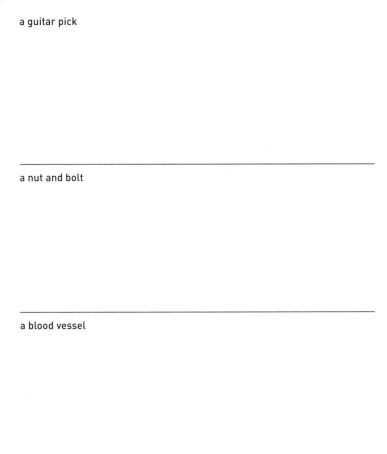

a domino | wooden beads

a saffron thread | tweezers

sequins

---

a snake scale

a casino chip

a rifle bullet

a watermark

a cocoon

barnacles

a woodpecker hole

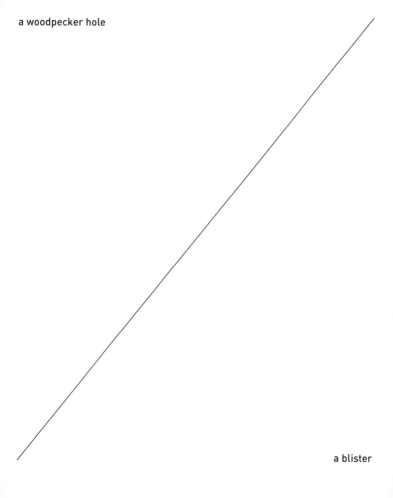

a blister

fish food

a jelly bean

---

wine dregs

an inch of rain

———————————————————————————————

a campaign button

an alfalfa sprout

---

a fortune in a cookie

---

a shot glass

silver dollar pancakes

a shrunken head

a tater tot

---

bubbles in bubble wrap

a price tag

---

a toothpaste cap

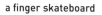
a finger skateboard

a seashell

a winning lottery ticket

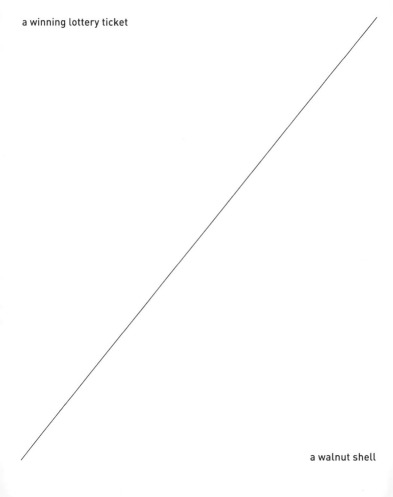

a walnut shell

an animal cracker

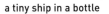
a tiny ship in a bottle

a porcupine quill

a spool of thread

eyelashes

a garden gnome

a carrot stick

a razor blade

a coffee stirrer | a computer memory stick

strands of cotton candy

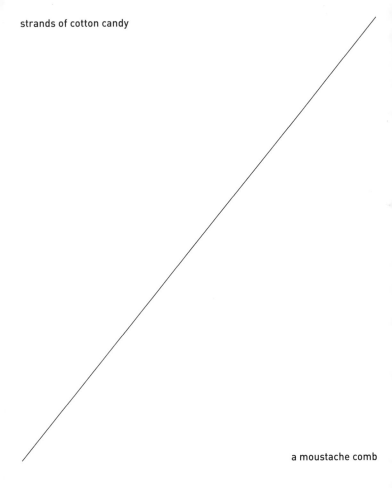

a moustache comb

a refrigerator magnet

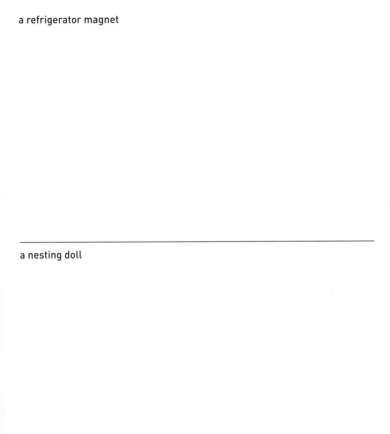

a nesting doll

knick-knacks

a branch of a bonsai tree

a bottle opener

a coat hook

_____

the narrowest part of an hourglass

a nose ring

---

pool chalk

a reflection from a mirror ball

a bus transfer

_____

a disposable razor

an oboe reed

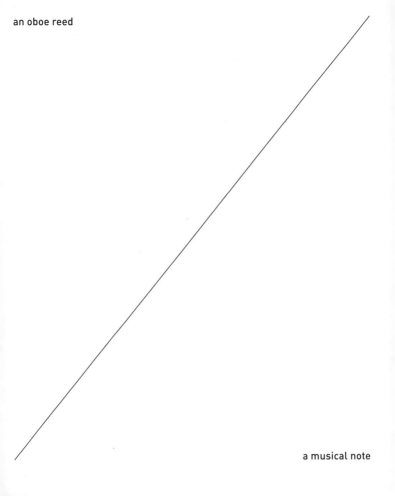

a musical note

an engineer on a model train

the straw that broke the camel's back

a fuse

a gingerbread man's hands

paintbrush bristles	an incense cone
a sweet gum ball	a cube of Swiss cheese

a discrete tattoo

a tiny robot

a compass dial

a smiley face

a spin top

---

a crystal shard

fish gills

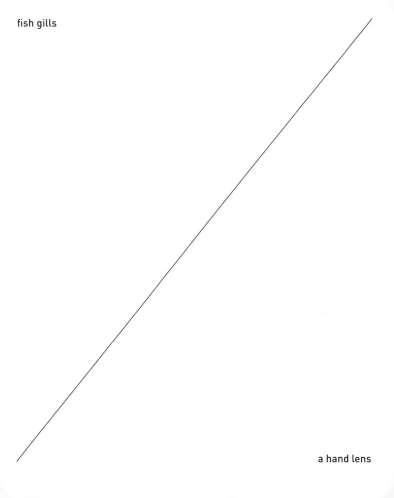

a hand lens

a pile of ashes

---

a fossilized impression of a fish

---

a rubber stamp

a scratch-n-sniff sticker

a ring box

gum under a desk

a quill tip

_____

one degree hotter

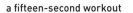

a fifteen-second workout

a "Made in China" label

---

a bacon bit

---

a piece of tape on a wall

a name written on the inside of underwear

_____

a modem activity light

a firefly at dusk

confetti

a gumdrop

---

a tickle

a cowlick | a drill bit

a mosaic tile

a file on a Swiss army knife

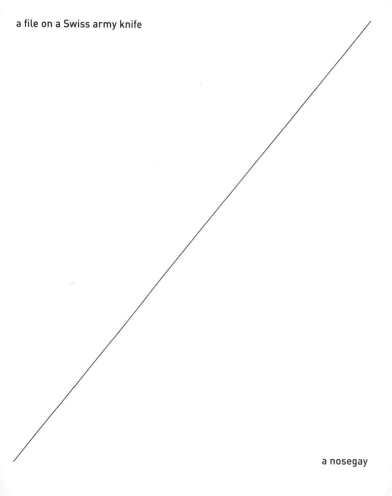

a nosegay

a light switch

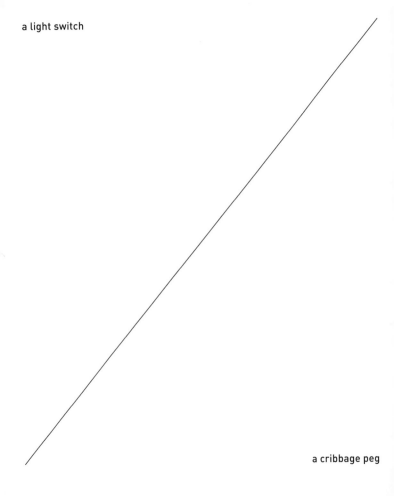

a cribbage peg

static electricity

a thermostat dial

a rough texture

the mouth of a cola bottle

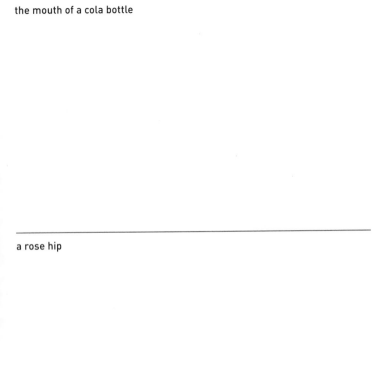

a rose hip

olive pits

---

a rip in a carpet

a doorbell buzzer | a dashboard statue

earplugs

_____

a tube of lip balm

a pineapple chunk

_____

a perfume sample

a dog whistle	a Christmas tree ornament
a frank and a bean	a bar code

an eyedropper

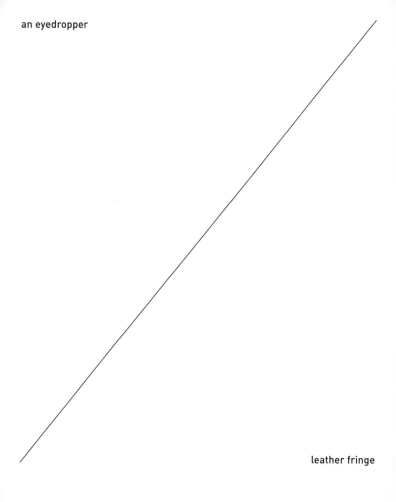

leather fringe

a souvenir pen

a merit badge

a cocktail umbrella

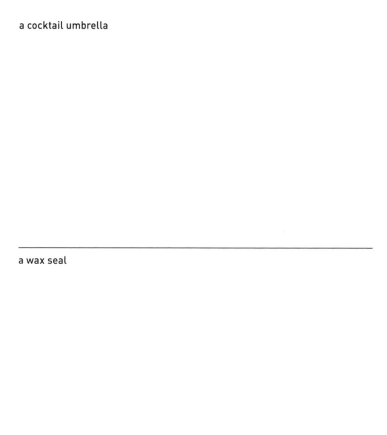

a wax seal

googly eyes

a pat of butter

a cherry blossom

a little devil

a bacteria

a bike bell

a bud vase

a rivet

a toy boat anchor

a knuckle

a trail of bread crumbs

a nap

a money clip

---

a potato eye

---

a cicada shell

a Chihuahua puppy

a fly-fishing lure

---

a slight tremor

packing peanuts | a reading light

a scrap of a treasure map

a dog treat

a dreidel

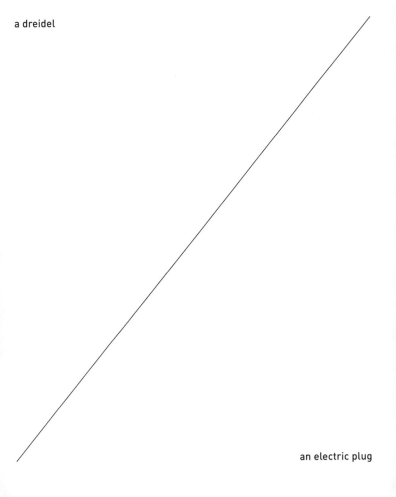

an electric plug

a cotton ball

a canary beak

a glimpse

a wedding cake topper

coconut flakes

granola

a jellyfish tentacle

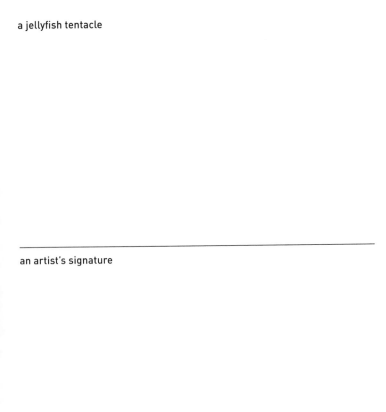

an artist's signature

a sand dollar | a finger bandage

an owl pellet | a lump of coal

a terrarium in a jelly jar

a dentist's hand mirror

---

a deep-fried grasshopper

a bubble pipe

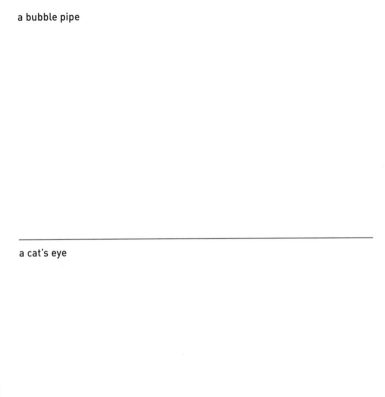

a cat's eye

a scorpion

a fishbowl castle

finger cymbals

a pilot light

an arrowhead

a drip | a caption

a garlic clove

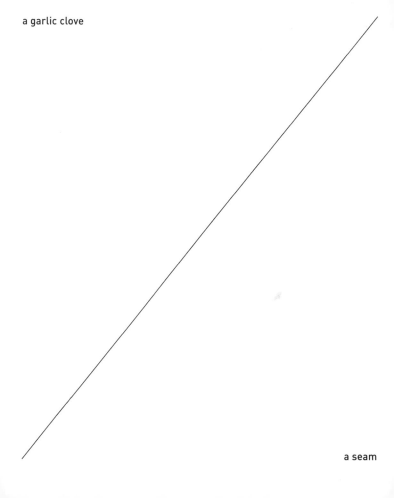

a seam

a bouncy ball	an ice cube
broken chalk	a speck of dust

saltwater taffy

a talk bubble

---

shoe tread

---

a golf ball

a bindi

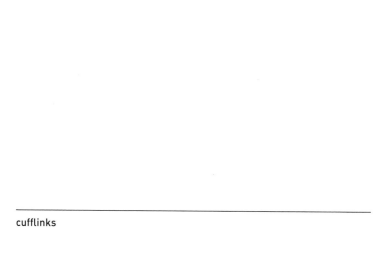

cufflinks

a monogram on a handkerchief

a hat pin

an evil eye

a leprechaun's belt buckle

mechanical pencil lead

a hand buzzer

a carabineer

a hood ornament

a monocle | ticker tape

a teddy bear's nose

_____

a strand of dental floss

a diamond in the rough

a decoder ring

a hieroglyph

an X-ray of a finger | a teacup handle

a pipe cleaner | mistletoe

a cowboy spur	a rubber gasket
a shower curtain hook	a travel shampoo bottle

a pocket first aid kit

a driver's license photo

---

a snow globe from Paris

a number written on a matchbook

_____

a twist tie

_____

houndstooth

a fuel gauge | a wonton

kindling | a peck on the cheek

a gecko

_____

a fang

_____

a trigger

moss on a rock

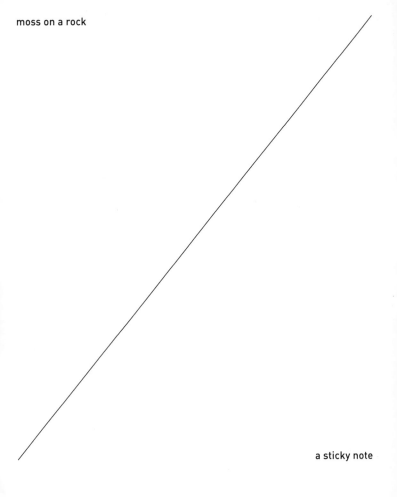

a sticky note

lock-picking tools | a poison dart

a crab claw

---

a round peg

---

orange zest

a solar cell

---

a honeysuckle blossom

an origami hedgehog

rock candy

lox

Easter grass

---

a foothold on a climbing wall

a radar blip

---

a foam design in a latte

---

yeast

a rollerblade wheel | the last bite of donut

a pressure cooker weight | a pencil sharpener

a Lilliputian

a graduation tassel | chain mail

a skipping stone

gingerroot

an element on the periodic table

---

a scrimshaw of a narwhal

"OK" in Morse code

a gate latch | a sink drain

a pig's tail | an Elvis keychain

a sideburn

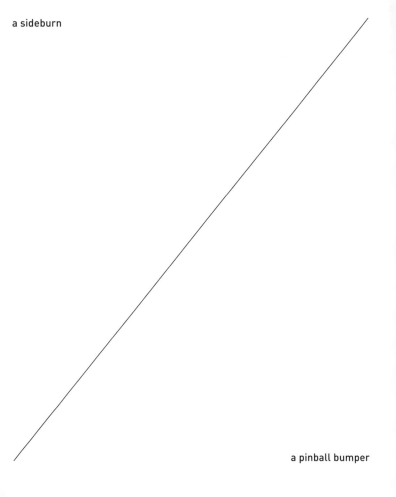

a pinball bumper

a nightlight

a two-word crossword puzzle

a snake rattle

a wire barb

---

an answering machine cassette

a magic bean

a smoke bomb

a doodle

a wheat berry | a dovetail joint

---

a tire patch | a pulley

a receipt | a 45 rpm record label

sunspots

---

an ampersand

---

photo corners

a water hose nozzle

the motor of a remote control plane

a pom-pom on a winter hat

_____

a jeweler's tool kit

a crochet stitch

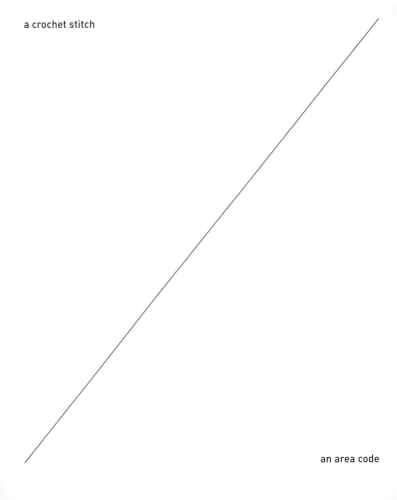

an area code

a dirt road on a highway map

a lavender sachet	a succulent clipping
a medal of honor	a spaghetti strap

a whiff

---

a pop-top on a soda can

a nail hole

mortar between bricks

a friendship bracelet

a spot on a leopard

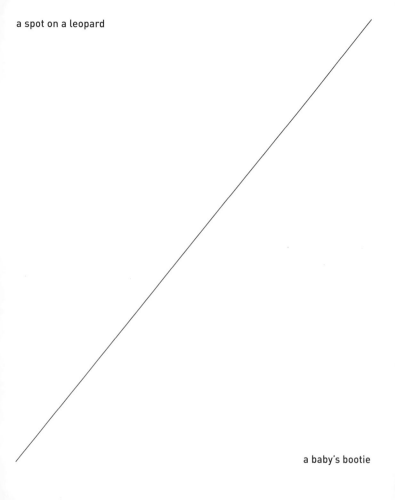

a baby's bootie

a heartbeat

---

a Chinese soup spoon

a reflection in sunglasses

a burr

---

emoji

---

a pepperoni

a coxcomb

---

a message from a homing pigeon

PENGUIN BOOKS

THRUSH GREEN

Although 'Miss Read' wishes to remain anonymous she says she is a teacher by profession who started writing after the Second World War, beginning with light essays written under her own name, mainly for *Punch*. She writes on educational and country matters for various journals, and also works as a scriptwriter for the B.B.C.

Her hobbies are theatre-going, listening to music, and reading. She is married, with one daughter, and lives in a Berkshire village. She has published many books, including *Village School* (1955), *Village Diary* (1957), *Thrush Green* (1959), *Winter in Thrush Green* (1961), *Miss Clare Remembers* (1962), *Fairacre Festival* (1968), *News From Thrush Green* (1970), *Tyler's Row* (1972), *The Christmas Mouse* (1973), *Further Afield* (1974), *Battles at Thrush Green* (1975) and *No Holly for Miss Quinn* (1976). In addition she is the author of two books for children, *Hobby Horse Cottage* and *Hob and the Horse-bat*, and The Red Bus series for the very young. (Many of 'Miss Read's' books have been published in Penguins.)

THRUSH GREEN

By 'Miss Read'

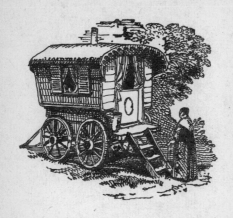

ILLUSTRATED BY J. S. GOODALL

PENGUIN BOOKS

IN ASSOCIATION WITH

MICHAEL JOSEPH

Penguin Books Ltd, Harmondsworth, Middlesex, England
Penguin Books, 625 Madison Avenue, New York, New York 10022, U.S.A.
Penguin Books Australia Ltd, Ringwood, Victoria, Australia
Penguin Books Canada Ltd, 2801 John Street, Markham, Ontario, Canada L3R 1B4
Penguin Books (N.Z.) Ltd, 182–190 Wairau Road, Auckland 10, New Zealand

—

First published by Michael Joseph 1959
Published in Penguin Books 1962
Reprinted 1967, 1970, 1977

—

Copyright © 'Miss Read', 1959

—

Made and printed in Great Britain
by Hazell Watson & Viney Ltd,
Aylesbury, Bucks
Set in Linotype Pilgrim

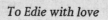

To Edie with love

Contents

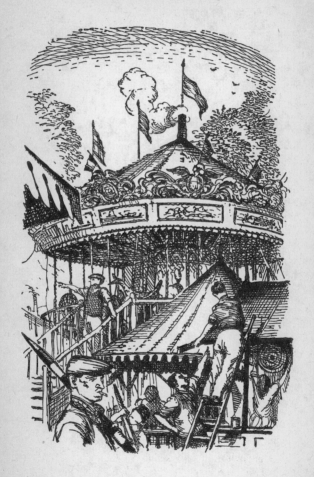

1. The Day Begins

As soon as he opened his eyes the child remembered, and his heart soared. This was the day he had waited for so long – the day of the fair.

He lay there for a minute, beneath his tumbled bedclothes, savouring the excitement. His mind's eye saw again, with the sharp clarity of a six-year-old, the battered galloping horses with flaring nostrils, the glittering brass posts, twisted like giant barley sugar sticks, the dizzy red and yellow swingboats and the snakes of black flex that coiled across the bruised grass of Thrush Green waiting to ensnare the feet of the bedazzled.

His nose tingled with the remembered scent of the hot oily smell which pulsed from the blaring roundabout and the acrid odour of his own hands, faintly green from clutching the brass post so tightly. In his head rang the music of the fair, the raucous shouting, the screams of silly girls in swingboats, the throbbing of the great engine which supplied the power and, over all, the head-hammering mammoth voice which roared old half-forgotten tunes from among the whirling horses of the roundabout.

At last – at last, Paul told himself, it was the first day of May! And at this point he sat up in bed, said 'White Rabbits!' aloud, to bring luck throughout the coming month, and looked eagerly out of the window into the dewy sunshine which was beginning to shimmer on Thrush Green.

And then, with a horrid shock, the child remembered something else. His heart stopped singing and dropped like a lark to the ground. Would he be able to go? Could he? Would he?

Frantically he clawed at the buttons of his pyjama jacket, tore it open, and surveyed his chest with agonized anxiety.

'The rash has almost gone,' young Doctor Lovell had said to Aunt Ruth the night before. 'If his temperature stays down, I don't see why he shouldn't have an hour at the fair.'

Aunt Ruth had smiled at Paul who had bounced up and down on the mattress with excitement.

'But you've got to take it quietly, young man,' went on Doctor Lovell, 'otherwise, no fair!'

They had left the child in bed and gone downstairs to the cool hall. The front and back doors of the pleasant old house stood hospitably open and the low rays of the setting sun crept in through the back door with the fragrance of the wallflowers which lined the garden path.

'He'll be so pleased if he can go,' said the girl. 'They say that this will be the last time the fair comes here.'

'Oh, you've heard that too?' observed Doctor Lovell. 'Evidently the old lady who runs the thing – Mrs Whatsit –' He snapped his fingers and cocked his long dark head sideways in an effort to remember.

'Mrs Curdle,' prompted Ruth. 'The great Mrs Curdle. Why, I remember her when Joan and I used to come here to stay as children! She always looked about eighty – and as tough as they make them!'

'That's it – Mrs Curdle. They were saying at The Vine last night that she's decided to sell the business.'

'It seems impossible,' said the girl, as they paced slowly down the short flagged path to the gate. 'And what her family will do without her to bully them all I can't think.'

The doctor opened the gate and stood outside. Ruth rested her bare arms on top and they gazed across Thrush Green to the half-dozen or so caravans which clustered at the further corner near the church some hundred yards

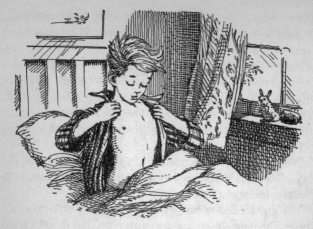

away. Most of them were gleaming modern beauties, flashing with chromium plating and fresh paint; but two of them were the traditional horse-drawn ones painted gaily with green and red, with yellow wheels and a bucket or two swinging from the axle, and in one of these, Ruth knew, lived the old matriarch who had ruled the fair for so many years.

In the still evening air blue smoke rose from the little tin chimney to the lime trees above. There was a faint whiff of frying onions, and a lurcher dog was sitting close to the caravan, his nose pointed expectantly upward. Nearby two skewbald ponies, tethered to the trees, cropped the new grass.

'Looks the perfect life,' sighed Ruth longingly. 'Just wandering from place to place. Nothing to remind you of things you want to forget –' Her voice trailed away and her companion looked at her quickly. She was uncomfortably pretty, gazing into the distance like that, he thought, and looked much better than she had when he had first met her six weeks before. Then she had been a pathetic little ghost, sitting listlessly in her sister's house, answering politely when addressed, with her heart and mind in some far-distant place.

Damn that fellow! thought young Doctor Lovell savagely, for the hundredth time. And I suppose she'd take him back again if he came crawling, blast his eyes! He fought down his useless anger and spoke equably. The calm evening gave him courage to speak more intimately than he had dared before.

'You will forget,' he assured her seriously. 'Look at the day ahead and never backward. You don't need a caravan for happiness, you know.'

The girl looked at him directly and gave a quick warm smile. The young man laughed with relief and raised a hand in farewell.

'I'll look in tomorrow morning,' he promised, and set off across Thrush Green to his own temporary home.

Thrush Green stood on high ground at the northerly end of Lulling, a small sleepy prosperous town, which had been famous in the days of the wool trade.

The town itself lay some half a mile distant, its gentle grey houses clustered, in a hollow, on each side of the twining silver river, like a flock of drowsy sheep. The streets curved and twisted as pleasantly as the river, but shaded by fine lime trees, now breaking into delicate leaf, instead of by willows, soon to shimmer summer through, above the trout-ringed reaches of the River Pleshy.

The High Street tilted abruptly to rise to Thrush Green. It was a short sharp hill, 'a real head-thumper of a hill' in hot weather, as old Mr Piggott, sexton of St Andrew's, often said. In the grip of winter's ice the same hill was feared by riders, drivers, and those on foot. Years before, a wooden handrail, polished by generations of hands, had lined the high pavement, but the town council had decided that it served no useful purpose and detracted from the charm of the stone-walled cottages perched high on the bank above, and when the handrail had become shaky with age it had been dismantled, much to the annoyance of the Thrush Green residents.

The green itself was triangular, with the church of St Andrew standing at the southerly point. The main road from Lulling to its nearest neighbouring Cotswold town ran along one side of Thrush Green, and a less important lane threading its way to half a dozen or so sleepy little hamlets, skirted the other side. Across the base of the triangle at the northern end ran a fine avenue of horse-chestnut trees, linking the two roads, and behind them, facing towards St Andrew's across the green, stood five sturdy old houses, built of that pleasantly sunny Cotswold stone which reminds one of honeycombs, golden afternoons, and warm and mellow bliss.

It was in the middle house of the five that Ruth Bassett was staying this spring. She had known and loved the house all her life, for it had belonged to her grandparents, and she and her sister Joan had always spent as much time as possible at Thrush Green, escaping from their parents' home at Ealing whenever they could.

It had been wonderful as children to exchange the small garden, the neat tree-lined streets, and the decorous walks in Ealing parks, for the heady freedom of Thrush Green and the big untidy garden that lay behind the old house. Sometimes they travelled with their parents, for their father visited his mother and father as often as his work would allow. But sometimes the two girls travelled alone from Paddington in charge of the guard and it was these journeys that they loved best. Their spirits rose as the train rattled westward, leaving the factories and rows of houses behind.

Whatever the season the country enchanted them. They would stand in the corridor of the lurching train, in the springtime, watching the broad fields of buttercups whirling by, glittering like the Field of the Cloth of Gold in the May sunshine. In the summer they kept watch for the gay boats on the river, the sunshades, the punt poles flashing with drops in wet hands, and the trailing plumes of weeping willow ruffling the surface. During the autumn the glowing beech woods, gold bronze and red, flared across the hills like a forest fire; and in the Christmas holidays the bare, quiet stillness of the sleeping countryside formed the prelude to the cheerful domestic bustle of Christmas which they knew would welcome them at their grandparents' home.

Their grandfather had died first. Ruth remembered him pottering about in the garden, a little doll of a man with fluffy white hair and a complexion as softly pink and white as a marshmallow. He had taken a great interest in Lulling's affairs, and the people of Thrush Green were reputed to set their watches and clocks by the old gentleman's punctual appearance at his gate each morning as he set off for his daily walk downhill to the town. He had been a fine cricketer in his day, and during his long retirement he had attended the modest matches at Thrush Green and those more important ones at Lulling's playing field, and those at the neighbouring towns.

One sunny June morning he had returned from his walk a little more breathless than usual after the stiff uphill climb. He had lowered himself into the sagging wicker chair in the shade of the lime tree and had surveyed the fresh beauty of the flaunting oriental poppies and irises which he loved so well. From the house came the welcome smell of lunch being prepared. He had nodded off in the drowsy sunshine, and when they had come to tell him that lunch was ready, he lay there, beneath the lime tree murmurous with bees, in his last sleep.

In the following autumn his widow had died too, and the house had been left to Ruth's father. By this time Joan had become engaged to Edward Young, a Lulling architect in partnership with his father. The two families had been friends for many years and, as a boy, Edward had always been at Thrush Green to welcome the two girls on their visits. He had been a stolid child, even-tempered and quite impervious to the Bassett girls' quips. Ruth had secretly thought him rather dull, but she had had to admit that he had developed into a kindly, reliable man, devoted to Joan and their one little boy Paul, and possessing a remarkably dry sense of humour.

The house on Thrush Green was offered to the young couple by Joan's father, who was compelled to stay in Ealing to be near to his business.

'But the day I retire,' he had threatened his young tenants with a smile, 'you are turned out into the snow on Thrush Green, don't forget! And I move in!'

Meanwhile the house remained much as it was in the grandparents' day. Joan and Edward had changed the dark paint to light and had removed the lace curtains which had shrouded all the front windows in their grandmother's time, but little else had altered, and when Ruth came down to stay, she still felt the same uplift of spirits as she stepped inside the cool hall, and still half-expected to see the pink and white old gentleman and his bustling little wife approach to welcome her.

She always slept in the same bedroom, the one which she had shared as a child with Joan, and the view from its window across Thrush Green never ceased to enchant her. If she looked left she saw the wider road to Lulling, with a few comfortable houses standing well back in leafy gardens.

The tallest one belonged to old Doctor Bailey, who had
attended to Lulling's ills for almost fifty years, and who had
known the Bassett girls since they were babies.

To the right, on the narrow dusty lane, lay the village
school behind a row of white palings. A stretch of mown
grass lay between the palings and the road and on hot days
the children left their stony playground and lay and rolled
on the grass just outside. Only if their teacher were with
them were they allowed to cross the dusty lane to play on
the greater green, for Miss Watson was a timid woman and
had no doubt at all that each and every pupil would be run
over and either maimed or killed outright if she were not
there to keep an eye on their movements.

Beside the school stood the little school house, and beside
that a row of small cottages. In the last lived old Mr Piggott,
the sexton of St Andrew's. As The Two Pheasants stood
next door to his house he was handy not only for his work
at the church on the green, but also for his only pleasure. He
had been a source of fear to the Bassett girls when they were
small. Always grumbling, he had threatened them with all
kinds of dreadful punishment if he had caught them walking
in St Andrew's churchyard or sheltering in the porch. Now,
bent and rheumaticky and crosser than ever, Ruth and Joan
found him a figure to be pitied rather than feared, but both
agreed that he was an evil-tempered old man and they felt
very sorry for his only daughter Molly who kept house for
him.

'It's a good thing she's got a job in that pretty little pub in
Lulling Woods,' Joan told her sister. 'At least it gets her
away from her wretched old father for most of the time. I
can't think how she puts up with him. She's so sweet and so
terribly pretty – she's bound to get married soon, I suppose.'

And then she had stopped short and had cursed herself
fiercely for mentioning marriage to Ruth just then. In the

silence which fell upon the room that dusky April evening Joan had cast a swift look at her sister's drawn face and had hastily changed the subject to the plans which she and Edward were making for a few days' holiday. Ruth had offered to mind Paul while they were away, and secretly looked forward to having the peace and comfort of the old house with only the little boy for company. Joan and Edward couldn't have been kinder, she told herself, since the blow had fallen upon her. They had offered hospitality, rest, companionship, and the tranquillity of Thrush Green, all combining to act as balm to a hurt mind and heart; but yet she craved, now that the worst was over, for a little solitude in which to make plans for a timid, sad return to life.

They had driven off on a sparkling April morning and within two days Paul had developed a high temperature and a rash on his chest. Old Doctor Bailey, who just lately had spent most of his time in bed, had sent his young assistant Doctor Lovell across to see the little boy, and Ruth, who had met him soon after her arrival earlier in the spring, had grown to like this quiet young man who had slipped so easily into the ways and the affections of the people of Lulling and Thrush Green. Even Mr Piggott had spoken a grudging word in his favour.

'Pity he don't stop,' he had said to Ruth, nodding across the green at the departing figure. 'The old 'un ain't too good these days. But there – he won't give up till his knifing arm drops off. Still keeps an eye on some of the old patients, ill though he be himself.'

A tapping at the bedroom window above had interrupted this conversation. Paul's woebegone face was pressed to the glass and Ruth had hurried back to the patient.

'All that's troubling him,' old Piggott had called after her, 'is whether he'll be fit to go to the fair!'

When Ruth awoke on the first day of May her first thought, as always, was of that nightmarish scene which had changed her life. The old accustomed horror engulfed her as her mind fought to turn itself away from such bitterness. But, to her surprise, the feeling was not so sharply cruel on this particular day. True, her mind shied from its remembrance like a terrified horse, but it did not plunge and toss, this way and that, in grief-maddened panic, in its efforts to shake off the devil that possessed it. It was as though a veil had been dropped between the dreadful picture and her mind's eye. She could see it all, down to the smallest detail, but the picture was dimmed, the impact was gentler, and her own feeling less agonized.

Could it really be true that time healed everything, Ruth wondered? For six weeks now she had woken daily to a sickening sense of loss and humiliation, and this was the first time that she had felt any lessening in the misery that engulfed her.

The clock of St Andrew's struck seven and she could hear movements from Paul's room across the landing. The first of May! The day of Thrush Green fair. No wonder that he was awake early. If the rash had gone and his temperature remained normal she felt sure that he would be allowed to go to the fair. Doctor Lovell would be along as soon as possible, she knew, to put the little boy out of his suspense.

She sat up and reached for her slippers. The sun was already striking rainbows from the dewy grass and gilding the roofs of the caravans on Thrush Green. As Ruth thrust her feet into her slippers she was struck once again by a second marvel. The thought of seeing young Doctor Lovell again had sent the faintest flicker of warmth into her sad heart. She sat on the side of the bed and considered this phenomenon dispassionately. To have the searing pain lessened at all was remarkable enough for one morning, but to find a little warmth among the dead ashes of her day-to-day existence was even more extraordinary.

Wondering and bemused, shaken with a vague sense of gratitude for mercies received, she went to the bedroom door. And clutching this crumb of comfort to her she made her way across the sunlit landing to see Paul.

2. The Great Mrs Curdle

MRS CURDLE heard St Andrew's clock strike seven as she lifted the boiling kettle from her diminutive stove. She had been up and about for over an hour, moving slowly about her caravan, straightening the covers on the bunk, shaking the rag rug, and even giving the brass on her beloved stove an early rub with metal polish.

The stove was the delight of her heart and had been built especially by a friend of her late husband's to fit neatly into the end of her tiny home. The top was of gleaming steel which Mrs Curdle rubbed up daily with emery paper, hissing gently to herself like a groom to a horse, as her busy hand slid back and forth, back and forth across the satin of the surface.

A circular lid could be lifted off and the fire then sent up its released heat to Mrs Curdle's kettle, stew-pot, or frying-pan. When the food was cooked, or the teapot filled, it could be kept hot by standing it farther along the hob, and frequently the top of the little stove was filled with a variety of utensils each giving off a rich aroma, for Mrs Curdle was a great cook.

The front of the stove was black but decorated with a great deal of brass. The knobs and hinges of the tiny oven door gleamed like gold against the jetty blacklead. Another

door, covering the bars of the fire, could be let down and
formed a useful ledge. It was here that Mrs Curdle heated
her great flat-iron, propping it up on its back with the ironing surface pressed to the glowing red bars.

But this morning the stove, despite its comforting warmth
and beauty, failed to cheer Mrs Curdle's troubled heart. She
had known, as soon as she had woken, that this was going
to be one of her bad days, for the burning pain in her back
and stomach had already begun to torment her.

'Dear, oh, dear!' had muttered poor Mrs Curdle, heaving
her back painfully from the narrow bunk. She had sat there
breathing heavily, for a full ten minutes, rubbing her
enormous stomach as rhythmically as she did the gleaming
stove top, and talking aloud to herself as was her custom.

'And only a morsel of fried liver and onions for me
supper! Never touched the cheese and never wetted me lips
with nothin' stronger than tea all yesterday. An' there's no
doubt about it – I'll have to turn it all in – turn it all in!'

She had gone slowly about her toilet, wiping her strong
brown face with a damp cloth and giving her neck and
magnificent bosom a perfunctory wipe afterwards. She
dressed herself in her black stuff dress, put on a dazzling
flowered overall, and pulled on a red and grubby cardigan.
Her hair she combed through carefully with soapy water
and braided it into shiny sticky bands, with two loops
hanging at each side of her head, each encircling an ear.
Gold drop ear-rings, the wedding gift of her husband, had
glittered against Mrs Curdle's weather-beaten cheeks for
over fifty years and these, with the exception of a gold
brooch with the word MIZPAH embossed upon it, were the
only ornaments that the old lady wore.

She had been a handsome girl, tall and beautifully pro-
portioned, with plentiful black hair and lustrous dark eyes.
And now despite her seventy-odd years and her great girth

she was still a fine-looking woman, with her jutting haughty nose and compelling gaze beneath the thick arched brows. She had treated her husband as an equal, in business affairs, in their domestic life, and as the father of their eight children. She had been as strong physically as he, for he was a slight man and they had shared the heavy manual work needed in setting up and taking down the equipment of their business. When he had died, as the result of a fall from the framework of his own swing-boats, at the age of fifty, Mrs Curdle had mourned him deeply. She had lost not only a husband, but her dearest companion and co-partner in a flourishing concern.

But Mrs Curdle had not mourned for long. The three oldest children were of an age to help in the fair, but there were five smaller ones, the youngest hardly able to walk and still needing the board across the doorway of the caravan to protect her from falling headlong down the three wooden steps that led precipitously to the great world beyond her tiny home.

She was determined that nothing should part her from the fair which she and her husband had built up over the years, with back-breaking effort. Two men, both distant relations of her husband's, remained to help her, and these two she ruled as strictly as she did her own struggling brood. Instant obedience was expected, and on the rare occasions when it was not forthcoming Mrs Curdle's mighty arm would swing, or her cruel tongue would lash, and child or fair-hand would meekly acknowledge his master.

Those who knew her but slightly marvelled that the children, as they grew old enough to earn their own livelihood, elected to stay with one so ruthlessly overbearing. But despite her matriarchal severity Mrs Curdle was scrupulously just and uncommonly warm-hearted, and her family adored, as well as feared her. She had no room in her

life for loafers, grumblers, or petty thieves; but an honest
man or woman who had fallen on evil times or needed
advice in trouble found in this indomitable old lady kindness, sympathy, and the wisdom born of experience.

Mrs Curdle had many friends and very few enemies in
the half a dozen or so counties which her caravan traversed
in the southern part of England. She was known to three
generations in villages and towns, and when the rumour had
gone round that the great Mrs Curdle was thinking of selling
her business and that the fair would be no more it came as a
sad shock. Grandparents in the water-meadows of Wilt-
shire, fathers and mothers in the grey Cotswold villages,
and little children playing among the wooded upper reaches
of the Thames Valley all felt the same pang of regret at the
possibility of this annual joy passing from them for ever.

'It doesn't seem possible,' old Doctor Bailey had said to
his wife, the week before Mrs Curdle's visit was due. 'May
the first, without Mrs Curdle on Thrush Green – why, the
whole idea's absurd! It just *isn't* May the first without
Mrs Curdle!'

'We shall miss the flowers,' said his wife. She was sitting
in an armchair in the window of the patient's bedroom
which looked across Thrush Green to the village school. The
doctor was comfortably propped up against his pillows in
the evening sunshine. He had spent the warm afternoon
pottering about in his garden, smelling the lilac, admiring
his tulips, and watching a blackbird flutter back and forth,
her beak full of wriggling insects for her nestlings nearby.

But now he was tired and quite content, as the April day
cooled, to be helped back into his comfortable bed and to
read or gossip lazily with his wife.

'Those flowers!' said the old man, shaking his head. 'A
bigger and brighter bunch each year it seems.'

Mrs Curdle's annual bunch of flowers constituted something of a problem in the doctor's house, for they were artificial and lasted for ever. They were indeed works of art, great mop-headed beauties made from finely cut woodshavings which curled into unbelievable shapes. Mrs Curdle had learnt this handicraft as a young girl and was an expert. When the flowers had been made she dyed them yellow, pink, orange, and scarlet and mounted them among evergreen twigs of laurel. They made a dazzling bouquet, not without charm, but the bunch which was presented each May Day by Mrs Curdle in person to the doctor was of such gargantuan proportions that Mrs Bailey was hard put to it to find a suitable place for it.

Each year Mrs Curdle asked to see how the previous year's bouquet had worn, so that the doctor and his wife were in honour bound not to destroy these offerings.

'Do you realize, my dear,' said the doctor, 'that we've had a bunch of Curdle blooms ever since 1915?'

'Forty-odd years with the top shelf of the pantry occupied,' commented Mrs Bailey. 'And then having to remember to unearth them before the day! Really, I shan't know myself.'

'I don't like the idea,' responded the doctor with vigour. 'To think of that caravan drawn up in some buttercup field under the lee of the same hawthorn hedge for ever, with grass seeding over the wheel-tops, and the shafts down, rotting – no, I tell you! It's against nature. Mrs Curdle's too game to let that happen. Surely, she'd never let it happen!'

But there was a query in the old man's tone and silence fell upon the room. Outside, the blackbirds scolded and the sound of children playing on the green, glorying in the first few outdoor games of spring, could be faintly heard. Mrs Bailey stole a glance at her husband. His blue eyes were gazing far away and his wife knew that he was thinking of that distant evening when he and Mrs Curdle had first met, on just such an April evening, many years ago.

Doctor Bailey was then a young man in his twenties, newly qualified and recently married and settled in this his first practice. The tall house on Thrush Green had been but sparsely furnished for the young couple had great aspirations but little money, and most of the furniture was solid Victorian stuff given by their parents. The large room to the left of the graceful hooded front door was young Doctor Bailey's surgery. Later, as his family came into the world, it was to be the dining-room and a new surgery was built at the side of the house, but when Mrs Curdle first knew him the doctor and his wife dined in a sunny little room at the back of the house, conveniently near to the kitchen.

They had been at supper on that far distant evening when Mr Curdle, white with panic, had drummed madly on the glass of the hall door. The little maid-of-all-work had been disdainful, telling the wild-eyed rough-looking man that Doctor Bailey had finished his evening surgery and was not at home.

At this the sorely-tried husband had broken into such cries of frustration and wrath that the good doctor had thrust aside his plate and gone out into the hall to discover what all the hullabaloo was about.

'It's me missus, sir,' had said Mr Curdle, clutching the doctor's arm. 'It's on the way – afore time. Ain't never seen her this way afore!'

'I'll come,' had answered the doctor, picking up his bag from the hall table. The maid had retired, tossing her head at the thought of such low people as them gyppos having the sauce to interrupt the master at his supper.

The two men had crossed the green to the small caravan. The husband was voluble with anxiety.

'This makes the fourth,' he had told the doctor, 'and never a minute's worry with any on 'em! Be as strong as a 'orse, me old gal; but never see her this way!'

The doctor had entered the tiny caravan which was stuffy and evil-smelling after the fragrance of the April evening outside. It seemed packed with humanity, for as well as the patient, writhing and moaning in the narrow bunk, there were two women, administering advice and pungent potions, as well as three small children.

'Get them all outside,' the doctor had said curtly, and the crowd had melted away leaving him with his patient and her husband hovering anxiously at the door. After a brief examination he had scribbled a note and handed it to the husband.

'Run across to my house with that and tell my wife to lose no time,' he said.

'What's it for?' stammered the man.

'For the ambulance. We must get her into the county hospital straight away.'

The man had vanished at once, but the patient had burst into hysterical screaming at the word 'hospital'.

'Ah, don't 'ee send me there, doctor dear! Please don't send me to that place, doctor. I'll die – that I will! I'll die!'

'You'll die if you don't go, young woman,' the doctor had said honestly. The straight words had shocked her into silence and she lay quietly until the ambulance had arrived. It was a high, dignified vehicle, the pride of Lulling Cottage Hospital, and the outcome of many fêtes and jumble sales in the neighbourhood.

Doctor Bailey never forgot that ten-mile journey to the county town. He had sat inside watching his patient, directing the husband who was now in tears, to sit in front with the driver. It was one of those typical April evenings, showery and sunny in turn. The sky was a purplish-grey with heavy storm clouds and against this background the young green of the new leaves gleamed goldenly. As the ambulance lurched along through the scented odd-coloured evening the doctor was struck, for the first time, by the memory of Millais' picture of 'The Blind Girl'. The artist had caught the same bizarre colouring exactly, and enhanced it by the addition of that unforgettable, glowing, auburn hair.

Young Mrs Curdle had clung pathetically to the doctor's hand throughout the journey. He had promised her that all would be well, that the hospital staff wanted to help and not to frighten her, and that if she did all that she were told the baby had every chance of being born alive and of flourishing. She had listened silently, tears rolling helplessly from her dark lovely eyes, but she knew, before the agonizing journey was over, that here was a true friend and counsellor.

The child had been born the next day after a gruelling period of pain. It was a delicate boy and the mother was ill for over a month after the birth. She was moved to Lulling Cottage Hospital where Doctor Bailey saw her each day and grew to like this gallant young woman whose spirits returned slowly with her strength.

No one could guess how much hospital life oppressed the girl. She lay in her bed on the veranda and gazed listlessly at the neat rose-beds, each trim bush bearing a tidy label with its name, and she craved for the sight of a spray of pale wild roses tossing in the fresh breeze on the open downs, for the splash of rain on her face, and the whistling of the wind through her hair.

She ate the grey tepid food on the clean white plates obediently, and yearned for the mingled smell of wood-smoke and hare broth and the clatter of her own metal spoon and platter. The one bright spot of her arid day was the visit of young Doctor Bailey. To her he was god-like. Without him she would have died, and her son with her.

Every Sunday her husband came from whichever of the nearby towns the little fair was working. He came dressed in his best black and sat, monosyllabic and ill at ease, among the white counterpanes, the flowers, and the rustling nurses.

Mrs Curdle questioned him sharply about the business and the children, but that done conversation languished, and each was secretly relieved when the visiting time was up and he made his sheepish farewells, too shy to kiss her before strangers and too loving to go without pain.

Early in the July of 1914 Mrs Curdle and the baby had joined the fair again in a windswept Berkshire village, but not before Mrs Curdle had given her thanks to the young doctor and promised to show him the baby on her next visit to Thrush Green at the beginning of the following May.

'And take care of him,' the doctor had said. 'He's a fine boy and I shall look forward to seeing you both next May.'

But it was not to be, for within a month war had broken out in Europe and the doctor was fighting in France when Mrs Curdle had called with her baby and the first of many bunches of lovingly-made flowers. It was Mrs Bailey, herself by now the mother of a young son, who admired the child and accepted the bouquet; and it was not until George Curdle (named after the King) was a sturdy child of five that he first saw the doctor who had helped to bring him into the world.

And now, on this May morning more than forty years from those far-off days, Mrs Curdle thought again of Doctor Bailey. She would go to him for medical advice, for the second time in her life. She had come to this decision slowly and painfully, and only at the promptings of prolonged and terrifying suffering.

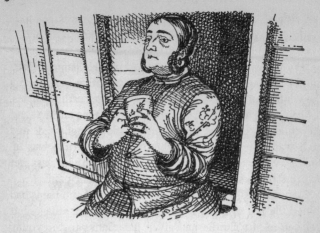

For months now the pain in her stomach had made her even more dictatorial than usual. Many a sharp word to her large family had called forth muttered blasphemies from growing grandchildren less willing to show the meek respect which their parents had done to the head of the tribe.

Old Mrs Curdle was too proud to consult her daughters, or even women friends of her own age, about her ailments. She suffered the burning pain, the nausea, and the headaches without complaint, and only her growing impatience and tired eyes gave a hint that she was not a healthy woman.

Secretly she had made up her mind that she was the victim of cancer. She had heard enough of this enemy to fear it, and she visualized this creeping evil groping about the tender members of her body with deadly tentacles. On one thing she was determined. If Doctor Bailey discovered a growth within her, then within her it would remain. Nothing, she swore, would be as terrifying to her as hospital and the surgeon's knife. She would carry her pain back to the caravan, and bear it as best she could, as she had done for so many months, until the good God released her from its clutches. She was used to it now and could settle down with it philosophically, like a mother with a bad-tempered child.

She took her cup of black tea to the doorway and settled down on the steps of the caravan. The air blew deliciously cool upon her face and the warm tea soothed her pain. The camp was astir. Water was being emptied on to the grass, young mothers pegged baby clothes on improvised lines, and over by the village school Mrs Curdle could see her favourite grandson Ben, George's only child, a boy of twenty, buying milk from the van which delivered daily on Thrush Green.

Her old heart warmed towards him. He was just like his father, just as tall, just as dark, just as quick and handsome. The old pang gripped her as she thought of George, as she always did when she came to Thrush Green, virtually his birth-place. His photograph, in uniform, stood in the very centre of the tiny mantelshelf. He smiled at her from it as he had smiled so often, and would never smile again. For George, her dearest, had been killed in France three weeks before the Second World War ended, and his timid little wife and young Ben had been left in Mrs Curdle's care.

She had turned all her fierce maternal love upon this child who returned her affection, and when his mother had been offered a second marriage by a grocer in one of the small towns which the fair had visited, old Mrs Curdle had insisted that Ben remain with her. This suited both the grocer and the colourless little woman who had once made George so happy, and thus it was that Ben was brought up by his grandmother.

She looked at him now as he brought back two bottles of milk across the dewy grass, and the pleasure which the sight of him gave her turned suddenly to unhappiness as a spasm of pain and sad remembrance gripped her.

Ben might look like George, but he'd never be the man his father was if he carried on as he had done during the last few months! Mooning about, sulking, answering back! Mrs Curdle didn't know what had come over him lately. Where was the fun they used to have together? Never heard him sing these days or crack a joke or laugh hearty.

Mrs Curdle sighed and watched him pass beyond one of the caravans. She struggled to her feet and swayed against the door as the pain stabbed her.

Ah, well! Another day to get through. Another day nearer the end of the poor old fair, she told herself, looking at the bustle around her. A pity for it to go. If young Ben were more like his dear father and had the life and go he used to have, why, she'd be glad to hand the reins over to him – but there, it was no good thinking of that these days.

She looked at the table in the dusky corner of the caravan. There lay the largest bouquet of wood-shaving flowers she had ever made. It might well be the last, she knew.

Tonight, after surgery hours, she would call, an annual pilgrim, on old Doctor Bailey and tell him all her troubles. And from that kind old friend she would, at last, learn her fate.

3. Ben Curdle Meets His Fate

BEN CURDLE walked back from the milk van, across the wet grass, a bottle dangling from each hand. He was conscious of his grandmother's morose eye upon him, and averted his own gaze. His dark young face looked surly, but his heart was bounding joyfully about in his breast like a clockwork toy.

He knew where she was! He knew where she was, he sang to himself! For two pins he would have turned cartwheels down the length of Thrush Green and back. This was the finest day in his life, the finest day the world had ever known. He had found his girl.

He had met her exactly a year ago, when the fair had visited Thrush Green. It had been a cold, blustery day, but lit with such warm radiance for young Ben Curdle that he would never forget it. He had seen Molly Piggott, first, very early in the morning. She had emerged from the cottage next to The Two Pheasants armed with a bucket and scrubbing brush, and had plumped herself down to scrub the red-brick doorstep. She wore a frock with blue flowers on it, Ben remembered, and a red woollen jacket. Her pretty legs were bare and she wore white sandals. She had a mop of curly hair as dark as his own, and when he had called 'Good morning' to her from the doorway of his caravan she had flashed such a smile at him that his heart turned over. The sleeves of the red jacket were thrust up above her elbows and the water from the scrubbing brush ran down her milky arm and trickled to the ground.

For a year now Ben had remembered her like that at will. They had spent three or four hours of that enchanted day in each other's company, and though Ben remembered it all and hugged the memories to him desperately, it was that first glimpse of her that stayed most clearly in his mind and had given him mingled comfort and torment for so many barren months.

At that time, and ever since she had left school three years before, Molly Piggott had been living at home, looking after her father, that crotchety widower, cooking his midday meal, her own life largely governed by his sexton's duties. In the afternoons, after washing-up at the shallow slate sink in the tiny scullery, she walked across Thrush Green to the Bassetts' house.

Here she ironed or mended linen, mostly for young Paul,

who adored her, until quarter to three, when Paul's after-dinner rest ended. It was then her duty and pleasure to get him up and take him out for an hour or so, returning to nursery tea, followed by a game, bath-time, and bed. Between six and seven she returned to her own cottage and spent most of the evening alone whilst her father drank gloomily in the pub next door.

Molly had been quite content with this placid life, despite the constant grumblings of the old man. Luckily, he was out of the house for a large part of the day, pottering about the church and churchyard, occasionally digging a grave and tidying it after the sad ceremony or ringing a wedding peal and sweeping up the confetti and gay little silver horseshoes afterwards. His demeanour remained exactly the same whatever the function. He hauled on his striped furry sally as each young couple emerged, starry-eyed, into the dazzling sunshine of Thrush Green, with the same gloomy expression of a disgruntled tortoise, with which he wielded his mattock to lift the first sod for some boyhood friend's grave. Life was sour for old Mr Piggott, and he made sure that everybody knew it.

The afternoon was the happiest part of Molly's day. She did her ironing or mending in the quiet stone-flagged kitchen whose windows looked out upon the garden in which old Mr Bassett had pottered and finally died. She loved this tranquil hour in the hushed early afternoon. Thrush Green was somnolent in its after-dinner nap, and the old house dozed around her. Paul was in his bed upstairs playing, looking at his books, or sometimes merely lying there in that blissful state between sleeping and waking, where dreams and reality merge imperceptibly and the cry of the cuckoo from the lime tree might well be the chime of the clock on the wall of the dream-room into which one has just floated.

Molly's kitchen was fragrant with the smell of freshly ironed linen and she felt her satisfaction mounting with the pile. Paul's small shirts and vests, his minute trousers and his handkerchiefs, bright with nursery rhymes, all received especial care. And later, as she sat in the low wooden arm-chair, with the needle flashing in and out of the clean clothes, she would plan the walk that she would take him when the time came to lift young Paul, warm and heavy, smelling faintly of Vinolia soap, from his rest.

In the winter they kept to the roads, or, if the earth were hard with frost they might play on Thrush Green with a bat and ball in view of Paul's home. Occasionally they walked down the steep hill to Lulling to shop for some-thing which Joan had forgotten. But more often they took the little leafy lane which led from Thrush Green to Upper Pleshy, Nod, and Nidden, the lane that threaded half a dozen or more sleepy thatched villages, like hoary old beads upon its winding string, before it emerged upon the broad high-way which led to Stratford-upon-Avon.

Sometimes their expeditions were more adventurous. Molly and Paul knew all the true joys that were within an hour's walking time of Thrush Green. There was the pond that lay, dark and mysterious, along the lower road to Lulling Woods, mirroring the trees that stood around it. Sometimes in the summer Paul had taken a bright wooden boat on a string and floated it there, beating at the water's edge with a fan of leaves to make waves. In the spring vast masses of frogs' spawn floated just beneath the surface, like submerged chain-mail cast there by some passing knight. And on one day of hard frost Paul and Molly had slid back and forth across the shining ice, screaming with delight, watched by a bold robin who sat fearlessly nearby on a low bare branch preening the pale grey feathers that edged the bronze of his breast.

There were other places that they loved which were accessible only in the summer. There was the steep path through Lulling Woods, cool as a cathedral, even on the sultriest day. There was the field path to Nod, where the grass brushed Paul's shoulder in high summer and he looked at marguerites and red sorrel at eye-level. A bower of brier roses guarded the final stile that led into Nod and, in later life, Paul never smelt that sharp breath-taking sweetness of the wild rose without remembering the languor and warm happiness of those golden afternoons with Molly Piggott.

She was the perfect companion for a little boy, placid, good-tempered, and ready to answer endless questions.

'Why can't I fly, Molly?'

'Would you be terribly, terribly sad if I died, Molly?'

'Why don't all animals have horns?'

These were a few of the simpler questions that Molly faced daily. When Paul started to attend Sunday school at St Andrew's and, later still, listened to Miss Watson's Scripture lessons at the village school, the queries grew more difficult.

'Did John the Baptist *always* have a headache?' he asked at tea-time one day.

'Never knew he had one,' said Molly equably, spreading jam for him.

'Well, he said he wasn't fit to stoop down and tie up shoe laces,' pointed out Paul reasonably, cutting the bread and butter energetically. And later on, as Molly tucked him into bed he had asked:

'Who is the Holy Ghost, Molly?'

Molly pushed her hair back from her forehead, screwing up her eyes in an effort to solve this teaser.

'I don't rightly know, Paul,' she answered slowly, 'but he was a friend of Jesus's.'

'What I thought,' answered the child, butting his head into the pillow, and, satisfied, was asleep in two minutes.

When Paul was five and had started school Molly feared that her services might not be needed at the house on Thrush Green, but Joan Bassett had reassured her. The two had been together in the big kitchen, one December afternoon, Molly with her mending and Joan icing the Christmas cake, while Paul rested upstairs.

'You know that Paul starts school in the New Year,' Joan had said, intent on her sugar rosettes, 'but we all hope you will stay with us for as long as you want to.'

Molly had kept her head bent above her sewing but her heart leapt at the news.

'He ends school at half past three each day, so that you can have tea with us as you've always done and help with the linen and run a few errands –'

Joan paused as she negotiated a tricky edge with her icing tool. Molly said nothing, speechless with relief. Joan wondered if the girl might have other plans and began again with some diffidence.

'Of course, I know you'll want something with more scope now that you're getting older, and we'd never stand in your way, Molly. You must feel quite free to go to any other post if you are offered one.'

'Oh, no!' Molly exclaimed from a full heart, 'I don't *ever* want to leave here!'

And, at that moment, she really meant it.

And so the winter months had slipped by, with Paul bursting from school at half past three and running home across the green bearing a paper mat woven erratically from bright strips, or a wallpaper bookmark still damp from the paste brush, as a souvenir of his day's labours.

He was ecstatically happy at the little school. Both

teachers he had known from babyhood. Miss Watson he saw but little, for she took the older children, and after morning prayers and a Scripture story she retired to her own classroom and was seen no more by Paul. But Miss Fogerty, the infants' teacher, he adored, and she began to share Molly's place in his heart. She had been teaching at Thrush Green school as long as the Bassett girls could remember and had not changed a scrap in all the years. Small and mousy, with very bright eyes behind gold-rimmed spectacles, she darted about the classroom and playground still wearing the silver pencil on a long chain about her neck that Joan remembered from her own childhood glimpses of Miss Fogerty.

Molly missed the companionship of the child on the afternoon walks. She often ran an errand nowadays for Joan at the time when she had formerly taken out Paul. She was a reliable shopper and Joan found that she could give her

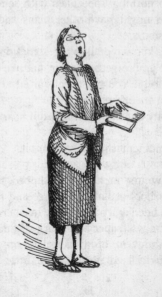

increasing responsibility in choosing food and drapery from the shops in Lulling. By Easter-time Molly was doing a large part of the catering for the household at Thrush Green, keeping an eye on the larder and making intelligent suggestions to Joan for the evening meal when Edward would be home.

Joan began to hope that Molly would indeed stay for ever, as she had so ardently promised. But on the day of Thrush Green Fair young Ben Curdle had walked into Molly Piggott's life, and by the time the harvest was being gathered, things had changed at the house on Thrush Green.

It had been a cold, wretched day that year for the first of May. The gusts of wind shivered the young lime leaves about the caravans and the sky was as grey as the canvas tent which housed the 'Marine Wonder' hard by.

Molly had spoken a few words, during the morning, to the dark young man who was busy erecting the scaffolding for the coconut shies opposite her cottage. She had liked him from the first moment that she had seen him when she was scrubbing the doorstep. She liked his soft voice and his crinkly, wiry hair and the odd shape of his dark eyes. If she had been drawing his face, she thought to herself, she would have put triangles for his eyes. Molly liked drawing and Miss Watson had often pinned her sketches on the schoolroom wall for her fellow-pupils to admire.

He had called to her when she emerged to go shopping for old Mr Piggott's dinner with her basket on her arm. He was squatting down in the wet grass, his hair upswept in the wind, looking intently at something on the ground.

'Come and see,' he invited, giving her a crooked smile, his head on one side. Molly had crossed the road and gone to look. A young frog, speckled and yellow, crouched between Ben's shoes, its throat pulsing, its starfish front feet turned in. For a dreadful moment Molly feared that he might kill it, as she had seen other stupid country boys do when they were displaying their manly bravado before the girls, but with relief and pleasure she watched him gather it in his grimy hands. He rose in one graceful movement and crossed to the railings of the churchyard where the grass grew tallest. He deposited the creature there and returned to Molly wiping his hands down his black corduroy trousers.

'Coming to the fair?' he asked.

Molly nodded, her face alight with mischief.

'And bringing a boy,' she quipped. Ben's face clouded and Molly was unaccountably stirred.

'Only a little one,' she said, laughing. 'Lives over there.' She nodded across to the Bassetts' house, hitched her basket further up her arm, and set off for the butcher's shop.

'See you later then,' Ben called after her; and Molly had trotted away, conscious of his eyes upon her back.

That afternoon Joan had asked her to collect some eggs from Dotty Harmer's and Molly had joyfully accepted the basket and the money, for the way lay close to the coconut shies.

Dotty Harmer was an eccentric old maid who lived alone in a ramshackle cottage in one of the meadows which bordered the path to Lulling Woods. Her father had been a history master at the local grammar school and Dotty had kept house for the old man until his death, when she sold their home, bringing some of the furniture, all the books, four cats, two dogs, and a collection of medicinal herbs to her new abode. The herbs flourished in her tiny garden, with roses, peonies, lilies, and carnations which were the envy of all the gardeners in Lulling.

Dotty concocted alarming potions from the herbs and these she pressed upon her unwilling neighbours and friends if they were unwary enough to admit to any slight ailment in her presence. So far, she had killed no one, but the vicar of St Andrew's had once had to call in Doctor Bailey as he was in agony with severe stomach pains, and had had to admit that he had taken tea and sandwiches with a peculiar and pungent filling, at Dotty Harmer's a few hours before. The Doctor had dismissed his troubles airily, diagnosing, 'Dotty's Collywobbles', a fairly common Lulling complaint, and had warned him about accepting further hospitality at that lady's hands.

As well as herbs and flowers Dotty reared some fine chickens and sold eggs to a few favoured friends. Molly often called there and enjoyed the old lady's garrulity.

That afternoon, as she had hoped, the dark young man was loitering by the coconut shies, as she approached.

'You busy?' he asked.

'Only going to get some eggs. It's not far,' she replied.

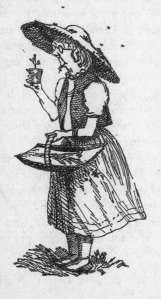

There was a pause. Molly did not like to stop for she felt that she might be seen from the windows of the Bassetts' house. Her father, too, might catch sight of her. He was in the churchyard, clipping the edges of the grass paths, but she was afraid that he might rise from the sack on which he knelt and shout at her if he caught her talking to this stranger.

'Can I come?' said Ben suddenly.

'Can't stop you, can I?' said Molly, swinging her basket and smiling at him. 'Come on then. We go this way.'

Between The Two Pheasants and the Piggotts' house was a narrow path which led gently downhill to the meadow where Dotty Harmer lived. Ahead, to the right, could be seen the massive leafy slopes of Lulling Woods, and the rushing of the wind in the turbulent branches could be clearly heard.

As they emerged from the passage-way between the buildings and dropped down the sandy path through the field they were suddenly sheltered from the tormenting wind.

'Peaceful, ain't it?' said young Ben, stopping still and looking at the view spread before him. 'Let's sit down.'

They sat on the cropped grass at the side of the path and talked slowly and shyly. Molly told him of her job at the Bassetts', about Paul, about her father, and about her daily round. He listened attentively, chewing a piece of grass, and nodding occasionally.

'But what do *you* do?' asked Molly. 'My word, you've got some luck, going about, seeing all these different places!'

'I like it right enough,' agreed the young man, 'but it wouldn't suit everybody.'

'It'd suit me,' said Molly forthrightly, then blushed as she thought of the construction Ben might put upon these bold words. She need not have worried. Ben answered her gravely.

'It's a rough life,' he said candidly, and he went on to tell her of the hardships and the discomforts and, finally, of old Mrs Curdle who ruled them all so firmly.

'But she's a grand ol' gal,' he asserted. 'She says sometimes she'll take me in as a partner. Ah, I'd like that – but there, you mustn't count your chickens.'

Molly rose and took up her basket.

'Chickens reminds me,' she said, and together they wandered across the meadow to the distant cottage, oblivious of the cold wind that whipped their hair and very contented in each other's company.

The children were streaming out of school when they returned to Thrush Green, and Paul flew across to her.

'That your young man?' asked Ben, looking at Molly with that engaging crooked smile.

Molly nodded.

'Reckon I shan't be jealous of 'ee!' said Ben. A harsh voice came floating upon the wind from a nearby caravan. It was Mrs Curdle's. She loomed, large and impressive, in the doorway of her home.

'See you tonight,' promised young Ben and hurried back to his duties.

Joan and Molly had taken the excited Paul to the fair as soon as it opened after tea. His bedtime was postponed time and time again at his own urgent pleading, but at last St Andrew's clock struck seven. Paul was led home, protesting still, by his mother, and Molly walked to the cottage which was her home.

She had spoken again to Ben, but only briefly, and he had whispered to her urgently:

'You coming back? On your own?'

'When I've give my dad his supper,' she promised him

swiftly. 'He goes off to pub soon as he's had it and I'll slip over again.'

She had been as good as her word and by half past eight she was back, her curly hair brushed into a dark cloud and her eyes shining. The blue and white frock which she had worn at their first meeting had been changed during the day for a yellow one, spotted with white, and she looked even more gipsy-like.

Ben put a young cousin in charge of the coconut shies and took Molly round all the side-shows of the fair. Molly had never had an evening like this before. They had turns on the swing-boats, roundabouts, switchbacks, dodgem cars, and helter-skelters, without pause, and Molly was dizzy not only with exhilarating motion but with the exciting companion-ship of this amazing young man.

At ten-thirty the fair began to die down, much to the relief of those residents on Thrush Green who were hoping for an early night. As the stalls began to pack up and the crowds started to thin out, Ben took Molly to a little jewellery stall close by the roundabout. A few people were having a last long ride and the raucous music blared out a sentimental ballad.

'Choose what you like,' said Ben to Molly, nodding at the dazzle displayed on the stall. There were necklaces, bracelets, ear-rings, and cuff-links, all cheap and tawdry in the cold light of day, but under the electric light and the flashing of the revolving mirrors of the roundabout nearby everything seemed exquisite to young Molly, dazed and bedazzled by a hundred sensations.

She chose a modest brooch in the form of a cornflower and Ben pinned it solemnly at the neck of the yellow spotted frock. The noise of the roundabout was deafening, but Molly saw Ben's lips move and thought she heard him say, 'Can you be true?' and she had nodded and smiled.

In the months that followed she often wondered about that half-heard question. Had he really said that? And, if so, had he meant to ask for her loyalty to him, or was he merely asking the silly sort of question that needed no answer, and which the voice from the roundabout was shouting too? Or had he said: 'Can *it* be true?' or had she misheard him altogether? Those four words were to puzzle and torment poor Molly for a whole year.

'I must get back to my dad. He'll be kicking up a fuss!' said Molly breathlessly. Ben had ambled at her side, past the stalls which were now packing up, to the cottage on the green.

They stood on the red-brick doorstep which the girl had scrubbed that morning.

'We're off first thing, so I'll say good-bye now,' said Ben. 'Had a good time?'

'Lovely,' breathed Molly. There was so much to say and somehow no words to say it. They stood in embarrassed silence for two long minutes, while the lights of the fair dimmed.

'Might get over if I can,' said Ben at last. 'Depends, though.'

'There's always the post,' suggested Molly.

Ben kicked moodily at the bricks.

'Bain't much of a fist at letter-writing,' he muttered.

From inside the cottage they could hear the scrape of chair legs on a stone floor.

'My dad!' whispered Molly in alarm. 'Good-bye, Ben. It's all been lovely.'

She reached up and gave his cheek a hasty peck. Then she turned the door handle and slipped inside the cottage before he could answer.

Bemused, young Ben wandered back to his caravan beneath the rustling lime tree; while, upstairs in the cottage,

Molly, in her petticoat, put away the cornflower brooch in a shell-encrusted box and prepared for bed with a singing heart.

But circumstances had combined against poor Ben. An alteration in the fair's accustomed route and his grand-mother's ill-health had prevented him from getting within visiting distance of Thrush Green. To his deep shame he could not write, for he had had very little schooling, and apart from signing his name he could do little. He had mastered the technique of reading, and, though he was slow, he enjoyed browsing through the newspaper and an occasional paper-backed thriller.

His pride forbade his asking a friend to write to Molly for him, and in any case he could not have put into words the deep feelings which rent him, and to ask for help in express-ing such emotions was unthinkable.

And so Ben suffered throughout the months that followed. Would he see her next May? Would she still be at Thrush Green? She might have got another job and gone away. Supposing another man had found her? This thought was so appalling that Ben's mind shied away from it only to be confronted by a worse horror.

Suppose she was dead? Killed, say, on the roads? Hun-dreds of people were each week. Or crippled? Or beaten by her horrible old Dad? Thus Ben tortured himself and roamed, restless and distraught, about his duties until it was no wonder that old Mrs Curdle, herself a prey to morbid fears, lost patience with her mooning grandson and com-pared him, more and more unfavourably, with that adored son buried in France. Ah, if only he had been alive, she told herself, throughout that worrying year, she would never have to think of giving up the fair, for there would have been a man – a real man – to carry on for her.

And now, a year later, Ben stood on Thrush Green once more. He had learnt that Molly still lived at the cottage, but not for all the week. Part of the time she was to be found at The Drovers' Arms on the heights of Lulling Woods where she was now employed for four days a week.

Ben had made his inquiries cautiously of the milkman. He had called at the cottage the night before but no one was there. He had asked a postman, going home from late duty, if he knew where she was, and he had not known. After that Ben had not dared to ask anyone too closely connected with Thrush Green for he feared that old Mr Piggott might hear of his inquiries and vent his annoyance on Molly. He had gone to bed much troubled, but was determined to track her down as early as possible next day.

The milkman had been most forthcoming.

'Ah! Up Lulling Woods, me boy. Helps in the house and then the bar Tuesdays to Fridays. Some chap takes over week-ends and Molly gets back then. Yes, still does a bit at Bassetts' now and again.'

He started up his ancient van with a roar, and shouted above the racket.

'You'll find her, me boy! Up Lulling Woods! She'll be in the bar till two, but free till six, I knows that 'cos I some-times gives her a lift into the town from there. You'll find her all right!'

He rattled off, the milk bottles clashing and clattering in the metal crates, as the van shuddered its way down the hill to the town.

And thus it was that at half past seven one May Day young Ben Curdle found the moon and stars joining the morning sun in a crazy heart-bursting dance over an enchanted Thrush Green.

4. Thrush Green Astir

By nine o'clock the sun was shining strongly from a cloudless sky. The light mists that had spread a gauze over the water meadows of the River Pleshy had now dispersed. As the dew dried in the gardens of Lulling the scent of narcissi and hyacinths began to perfume the warm air.

The birds were clamorous. Blackbirds alternately fluted and scolded as they bustled about in search of food for their nestlings. Thrushes ran to and fro upon the tender grass which bent beneath their fragile claws, stopping abruptly every now and again, to peer intently with a topaz eye at the ground before them. From gardens, woods, and parkland a dozen cuckoos called to one another with thrilling liquid notes.

The buds of the trees had cracked imperceptibly during the last week or so. Already the sycamores had frothed into yellow leaf and the elms, until recently covered with a rosy haze of tight buds, now showed a curdy mass of pale breaking leaves. Only the beeches it seemed were loth to emerge from their winter sleep, for still the long slender buds remained furled, upthrust and glinting in the sunshine like the bronze tips of spears.

On Thrush Green life was now well astir. Little Paul, still in his bedroom, and pyjama-clad, had finished his breakfast of boiled egg and bread and butter, and had watched his school-fellows running to school. Some had waved and called to him, and he had shouted back that his spots were gone but the doctor was coming, so he wouldn't be at school today.

Bobby Anderson, a lumpish child with a perpetually

damp nose, pointed to the end of the green where the fairground men were erecting scaffolding.

'Comin' tonight?' he bawled up at the window.

Paul nodded.

'Who said? Doctor?'

Paul nodded again.

'You better then?'

Paul nodded a third time.

'Oughter be over school then,' said his fellow-pupil
severely, and terminated this one-sided conversation by leaping upon a friend of his, knocking him to the ground, and
pummelling him in an affectionate manner. The school bell
rang out, the boys got up, dusted themselves down in a
perfunctory way and ambled across to the playground with
their arms across each other's shoulders, with never a backward glance at the little figure watching from the bedroom
window.

Doctor Bailey too was still pyjama-clad and had just
finished his breakfast in bed. The remains of toast and
marmalade lay on the tray on the side-table.

The sound of the school bell floated across Thrush Green
and Doctor Bailey put aside *The Times*, pushed his reading
glasses up on to his forehead, and gazed through the window
at the blue and white morning.

He could see a spiral of smoke from the chimney of Mrs
Curdle's caravan and a few gaunt spars as the men began to
erect the framework for the swing-boats. He could hear
their cheerful voices and the creak of timbers being hauled
and strained. There were heavy thuds as mallets rammed
supports into place, and the occasional high-pitched squeal
of a fairground child. Doctor Bailey sighed and drew up his
thin legs between the sheets.

If the rumours were true then this would be the last time

that he would hear the sounds of the fair. It seemed unthinkable that the first day of May should find Thrush Green as empty and quiet as on the other mornings of the year. What must the old lady be feeling, he wondered, as he watched her smoke curling delicately against the background of the fresh lime leaves. Where would she be next May? And where, for that matter, thought the doctor, would he be?

He faced this nagging problem afresh. For months now he had lived with it and he knew that he must find a solution, and the sooner the better. He knew, only too well, that he would never recover the strength and health which he had rejoiced in for seventy years. Well, he told himself, he had had a good innings and he supposed he should give up the practice and go and live in some confounded cottage where the roof was too low, and play bridge with other old dodderers every Wednesday afternoon, and do a bit of fishing when the weather allowed, remembering to wear a panama hat in case of sunstroke!

Pah! The doctor tossed his legs rebelliously and *The Times* slid to the floor. He'd be damned if he gave up! Give him another fortnight and he'd be back taking his surgeries and paying a few visits. There was still plenty he could do – it was just that he tired easily. No doubt about it, if he intended to continue in practice he must take a partner.

He heard the bang of the surgery door. It always caught the wind if there was a sou'-wester. He wondered how many patients young Lovell would have calling today. Doctor Bailey looked approvingly at the small silver clock on the mantelpiece. Only five past nine and that young man was well down to it! Yes, if a partner was needed then he would be quite content to have young Lovell in harness with him. He had watched him closely for six weeks, and he had listened to the gossip about his work. He was liked, not only for his youth, but for his quiet and sympathetic manner.

The older patients were delighted to find a new audience for their complaints, describing their symptoms with a wealth of nauseating detail which old Doctor Bailey would have cut short ruthlessly, as well they knew.

'Proper nice chap, that new assistant,' they said to each other.

'Hope he stops. Listened to me 'eart and that 'orrible rumbling in me stomach, as nice as pie, and what's more, give me a good bottle of medicine. Ah! A proper nice chap!'

A twittering, and a flash of black and white across the bedroom window, roused the doctor from his ruminations. The house-martins were up and doing, and so must he be, he told himself. It was going to be a perfect day. He would potter about in the garden and get some sunshine. Nothing like fresh air and exercise for giving you strength! He had told enough people that in his time, and he knew that it was true. He would follow his own advice and he would try and come to some decision about this proposal to young Lovell. He believed he would jump at the chance and somehow he felt that Thrush Green would suit him.

He thrust his long thin legs out of bed and stood up. Now he could see the bustle of fairground preparations and the sight warmed him.

The first of May again! There was always excitement in the air on Thrush Green then—and a bunch of flowers to come, he thought wryly, looking with affection at Mrs Curdle's caravan. As good a day as any to make a decision. Who knows, he might even ask that young fellow today.

With a light heart Doctor Bailey donned his dressing-gown and went, whistling, to the bathroom.

Mrs Bailey, sitting downstairs in the sunny little back room which had once been their dining-room, heard her husband whistling, and smiled. It was good to hear him so cheerful. He was getting stronger daily.

The whistling changed to singing and Mrs Bailey listened attentively.

> 'I think that we shall have
> A very, very lovely day :
> Very, very warm for May.
> Eighty in the shade, they say
> Tra la la –'

With an uprush of spirits Mrs Bailey remembered that night, over forty years before, when she and her husband had gone up to London to see *The Arcadians*. A visit to town was a rare treat in those days and they had enjoyed every minute. She had worn a lilac chiffon frock, she remembered, bought specially for the occasion, and shoes to match with diamanté buckles. What a shining, glorious time of life that had been, when everyone had seemed as young and as happy and hopeful as themselves!

Mrs Bailey set down the shopping list she was engaged upon and looked out into the sunny garden. An early butter-fly was abroad, hovering among the velvet wallflowers. They were so very lucky, Mrs Bailey told herself for the thousandth time, to have had their lot cast in such a pleasant place. Just suppose that the doctor's practice had been in one of the great industrial cities! She would have been looking upon a small soot-blackened garden, or – dreadful thought – upon no garden at all, and instead of Lulling's sleepy tranquillity they would have had to face the clamour and killing pace of life in a large town.

She had loved Thrush Green from the first moment that she saw it, and had grown fonder of it as the years passed; but she wished at times that it were easier to get to London, for she missed the theatre and the gay restaurants sorely.

Had London really been as wonderful as she remembered it just before the First World War, or was it the natural nostalgia, born of passing years, which made it appear so enchanting in retrospect? People nowadays seemed too busy for gaiety, and, what was worse, appeared to frown upon innocent enjoyment. Life was too dreadfully real and earnest these days, thought Mrs Bailey, and all the young people were middle-aged at twenty. And look at the dreary and revolting books and plays they wrote, about the most brutal and depraved creatures who didn't know their own minds, even when they had them!

The strains of *The Arcadians* floated from the bathroom strongly. Ah, there was fun for you, thought Mrs Bailey! If only people would realize that light-hearted and gay things were not any *less* significant than the violent and brutish, what a step forward it would be. Because a song, a book, a play, a picture, or anything created was gay, it did not necessarily follow that it was trivial. It might well be, mused Mrs Bailey gazing into the moving sunshine with un-seeing eyes, a finer thing because it had been fashioned with greater care and artifice; emotion remembered and trans-lated to give pleasure, rather than emotion remembered and evincing only an involuntary and quite hideous howl.

The gurgle of water from the bathroom pipes brought Mrs Bailey back to her duties. She looked again at her shopping list. Should she add liver, and make a casserole of liver and tomatoes for the doctor's lunch? It would be par-ticularly nourishing, and she could bake potatoes in the oven, which he loved. And while the oven was on she might as well make an egg custard, and perhaps she would put in a plum crumble-top to go with it. In which case, Mrs Bailey told herself, it would be sensible to make a really large amount of shortbread mixture so that she could make two tins ready for tea-time.

At this point in her housewifely manoeuvres Mrs Bailey caught sight of a wood pigeon on the lawn, its opal feathers glinting in the sunshine and its coral feet wet with the dew. All Mrs Bailey's good intentions dropped from her.

She would go out into this glorious morning. To salve her conscience she would walk down to Lulling and take her frock to the cleaners, and she would buy some ham and tongue and salad for lunch. It was far too wonderful a morning to spend in a hot kitchen, and against all natural laws on the first of May.

Despite her sixty-odd years, she ran upstairs with the agility of a girl, singing as she went:

> 'Very, very warm for May,
> Eighty in the shade, they say,
> Tra la la –'

And to the doctor, drying himself in the bathroom, she sounded as youthful and happy as when they had first heard that light-hearted ditty so long ago.

Across the green, in the infants' room Miss Fogerty was trying to teach the words of 'There is a Green Hill Far Away' to an inattentive class.

'But *why* hadn't it got a sitting wall?' persisted Bobby Anderson, his youthful brow criss-crossed with perplexity.

Above the noise of scuffling feet and the scraping of diminutive wooden armchairs Miss Fogerty attempted to explain that 'without' here meant 'outside', but before she could make herself heard, another child tugged at her arm and whispered urgently in her ear.

'But had all the other green hills *got* sitting walls? And *why* had all the other green hills got sitting walls?' clamoured Bobby Anderson vociferously.

Miss Fogerty clapped her hands for silence, the urgent child was dispatched hurriedly across the playground, the clock on the wall said nine-thirty and Miss Fogerty took her noisy rabble to the door in readiness for a physical training session.

And thus it was that Bobby Anderson was doomed to go through life with the hazy impression that the green hills of the Holy Land have, in the main, walls built round them – walls, moreover, not of the usual standing variety, but of a mysterious type called 'sitting'.

Old Mr Piggott leant over the iron railings of St Andrew's and surveyed the activity of the fair with a morose countenance.

'Goin' to keep fine?' inquired a brawny man, wielding an oil rag over the traction engine. He jerked a massive black thumb at the shimmering view behind him.

Mr Piggott was not to be wooed by honeyed words. He didn't hold with the fair and he didn't care who knew it.

'Can pour down for all I cares,' grunted old Piggott sourly. 'Might drown some o' your durned racket later on!'

''Ere, 'ere! 'Oo's 'urtin' you!' began the oily man truculently. He doubled his great fists, stepped down from the wheel of the engine, and advanced threateningly towards Piggott.

Mr Piggott stepped farther back from the railings, out of arm's reach, but he did it in a carefully casual manner to show that he was not intimidated. From a safe distance he replied.

'Two churchings at six-thirty,' he grumbled, 'and all that blaring racket goin' on outside. 'Tisn't reverent, I tell 'ee!'

And spitting forcefully into the laurel bushes, making a swift, flashing arc over the remains of one Ann Talbot, Virtuous Wife, Devoted Mother, and Esteemed Friend, he retired towards the protection of the church while the going was good.

5. Doctor Lovell's Patients

YOUNG Doctor Lovell was interviewing his last patient in the surgery, and finding it heavy going.

Ella Bembridge was a formidably hearty spinster of fifty-five who had lived, with a wilting friend of much the same age, in a small cottage on the Lulling corner of Thrush Green for the past ten years. It was generally agreed that Ella ruled the roost and that 'poor Miss Dean' had a pretty thin time of it.

Deborah Dean had been nicknamed Dimity, so long ago that the reason for the diminutive had been lost in the mists of time. Now, at the age of fifty-odd, the name was pathetically incongruous, calling up as it did someone fresh, compact, and sparkling, with an air of crisp, but old-world domesticity. Dimity nowadays resembled a washed-out length of grey chiffon, for she was a drooping, attenuated figure with lank, mouse-grey locks and a habit of dressing in shapeless frocks, incorporating unpressed pleats and draped bodices, in depressingly drab shades. Doctor Lovell, who knew both women slightly, suspected that she was brow-beaten by the dominating Ella now before him, and would have liked to try the effects of an iron tonic on Dimity's languid pallor.

He was beginning to wonder just how quickly he could bring Miss Bembridge's monologue to a close. She had come to consult him about a skin complaint affecting her hands and arms.

'I said to Dimity, "Looks like shingles to me. Better go and see the medico, I suppose, for all the good that'll do!" ' Here Miss Bembridge laughed roguishly and Doctor Lovell felt positive that she would have dug him painfully in the ribs had not the large desk providentially stood between them. He gave a faint smile in acknowledgement of this witticism, and glanced across the shimmering summer glory of Thrush Green to the Bassetts' house.

Miss Bembridge followed his gaze.

'I thought I might have picked up something from young Paul. Dim and I were there to tea a day or two ago and then the little horror came out in some repulsive rash or other. Not that I'm saying a word against Ruth! Heaven knows she's had enough to put up with, and naturally her mind is full of things other than a child's rash, but I do think it was just the *teeniest* bit careless to invite us there when the child was infectious.'

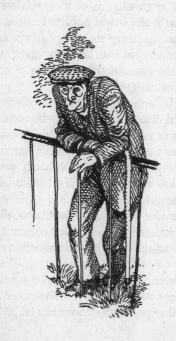

Doctor Lovell rose impatiently. His lean young face still wore a polite professional smile, but it was a little strained.

'Paul's rash,' he said steadily, 'did not appear until after your tea party. I was called in as soon as it was found.' He felt his dislike of this tough ungainly woman growing minute by minute. She had sat there for almost a quarter of an hour, her massive legs planted squarely apart to display the sturdiest pair of knickers it had ever been Doctor Lovell's misfortune to observe. In shape and durability they had reminded the young man of his father's Norfolk breeches used in the early days of cycling, and the silk shirt and Liberty tie added to the masculine impression.

It was an odd thing, mused Doctor Lovell, that it was Ella who was the artistic one of the pair. Dimity ran the house, it appeared, and it was her slender arms that bore in the coal scuttles, the heavy shopping baskets, and the laden trays, while Ella's powerful hands designed wood-blocks, mixed paint, and stamped the lengths of materials which draped their little cottage.

Occasionally Ella took the train to town with a portfolio of hand-blocked patterns, and usually she returned, blown but jubilant, with a few orders from firms who appreciated her strong shades of olive green, dull beetroot, and dirty yellow madly ensnared in black mesh. It was the paint, Doctor Lovell had surmised, which was causing the present rash on his patient's hands, and he had given her a prescription for a curative lotion and recommended the use of rubber gloves for a few days whilst handling her artistic materials. She had clutched the prescription in a pink spotty hand and had continued to sit stolidly in the chair. Poor Doctor Lovell, who was not yet completely versed in getting rid of lingering patients, resigned himself to another few minutes of Miss Bembridge's comments, delivered in a

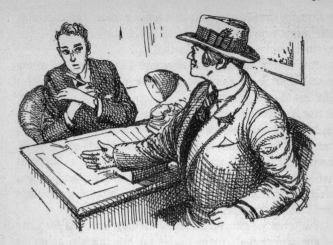

booming voice that would have been an asset in a ship-wreck. He had heard all about Miss Dean's fancied ail-ments after he had listened to the more pressing ones of Miss Bembridge, and he felt more and more like the unfortunate Wedding Guest who encountered the Ancient Mariner.

From outside came the sweet scent of the old-fashioned pheasant's-eye narcissi which Mrs Bailey massed against the wall beneath the surgery window, and the thump of Ben Curdle's mallet as he rammed home stake after stake. Doctor Lovell longed to be out in the freshness of Thrush Green's morning, but Miss Bembridge continued remorselessly.

'I tell her a good blow is what she needs. Get rid of the cobwebs. But no, every afternoon she says she must have a rest on her bed! Unhealthy, I tell her. But then, dear old Dimity always was a one for imagining she'd every ill under the sun. This back-ache now, she complains of –'

Doctor Lovell cut her short.

'Too much lifting, I expect. You'll have to see she gets

help with the heavy work. And tell her to call one morning.
I'll have a look at her.'

Miss Bembridge looked startled.

'Oh, there's nothing *really* wrong! That's what I'm trying
to tell you. Sheer imagination! Now, my hands are quite a
different kettle of fish –'

He had let her run on for one more minute exactly, his
eye on the round silver clock which had been Mrs Bailey's
mother's. It was then that Ella Bembridge had begun the sly
comments about Ruth Bassett's shortcomings as an aunt
which had made Doctor Lovell realize, with sudden passion,
that he could not bear to remain in this wretched woman's
presence for one split second more.

The cries of the junior class as they emerged into the
stony playground, there to bound breathlessly about as
galloping horses, reminded the doctor that it must now be
Miss Watson's physical training session and therefore almost
ten-thirty. He strode resolutely to the surgery door and held
it open.

'I mustn't keep you,' he said firmly, and watched Miss
Bembridge heave her bulk from the armchair, cross the
threshold, and depart, still booming and not a whit
perturbed, down the flagged path.

Doctor Lovell returned to the surgery to tidy his papers,
shut drawers and files, and collect his bag.

He closed the surgery door behind him and stood for one
minute savouring the fragrance of the May morning. The
air was cool and sweet. A spiral of blue smoke curled from
Mrs Curdle's gaily painted caravan, the children laughed
and called from the school yard, and on the highest point
of Doctor Bailey's roof a fat thrush poured out a stream of
shrill-sweet trills, his speckled breast throbbing with the
ardour of spring.

No less enchanted, young Doctor Lovell went through the

gate, his eyes upon the house where Ruth and Paul were to be found, and, crossing the shining grass of Thrush Green, prepared to make the first visit of the day.

Paul was standing on his head on the pillow of his bed. His pyjama-clad legs rested comfortably against the wall, and, apart from a slight discomfort of the neck, Paul was feeling very pleased with himself.

He had remained poised in this upside-down position for a full minute and this was easily the longest time he had managed so far. The room, he observed, really looked much more attractive this way, and the colours were definitely brighter. This fact so interested him that he lowered his legs with a satisfying bounce and looked again at his surroundings the right way up. They certainly looked duller. He adopted his former topsy-turvy position and gazed with fresh rapture at his transfigured world.

An early fly hovered around the central light and Paul wondered how it must feel, swooping aimlessly here and there. Surely the ceiling would seem like the floor to the fly, and he would think it the most ordinary thing in the world to have chairs and dressing-tables and tallboys hanging from the ceiling. Paul pondered about this until the crick in his neck caused him to drop his legs, climb off the bed, and wander to the window.

The school playground was empty and he wondered what his friends were doing under the red-tiled roof of the village school. A pigeon rattled out from the chestnut tree nearby and flew across to the school, its coral claws gripping the ridge of tiles as it landed. Paul caught his breath with envy. To be able to fly – just like that! Could anything be more wonderful than flying from roof to roof, from wood to wood, over fields and rivers, looking down upon Thrush Green and the whole of Lulling's chimney-pots? Why, if that pigeon peeped through a crack by his curling claws he might see all the children at their lessons!

It was a pleasant thought, and Paul turned it about in his mind as busily as his fingers were now twisting and un-twisting the bone acorn which hung at the end of the window-blind's cord.

He would like to be a giant bird, decided Paul, as he watched the pigeon. He would be so strong that he could lift the roofs right off all the houses in Lulling and then fly over the town and see everything that was happening inside. Aunt Ruth had read him the story of *The Princess and the Swineherd* and he remembered the magic saucepan which allowed the princess to know just what was cooking in every house in the kingdom. Paul thought his idea was a better one. Much better to see than to smell, decided Paul, twirling the blind cord. He would lift the school roof first.

Down below him he would see the round heads of his friends, black and brown and yellow, with here and there a bright hair ribbon. He would see the long wooden desk-lids and the plaited wicker circle which was the top of the waste-paper basket, and Miss Watson, curiously fore-shortened, standing by the blackboard. It must be past ten o'clock Paul reckoned, so that she would be taking a geography lesson on this particular morning. The map would be hanging over the easel, giving out that faint oily smell which always emanated from it as soon as it rolled, released, from its bright pink tapes. From his lofty vantage point he would listen to the far classroom sounds – the scuffling of fidgeting feet, an occasional cough, the lilt of Miss Watson's voice, and the tap-tap of her pointer against the map. He would replace the roof, silently, magically, as easily as slipping the lid back on to a box, and fly over to St Andrew's Church.

What would he find there, Paul wondered, gazing through the bedroom window to the building which loomed large behind the clustering caravans, against the dazzle of the morning sky. Probably only Mr Piggott would be in the church at this time. How small he would look from such a high roof! Paul could see him, in his mind's eye, shuffling slowly up and down the long nave with the pews stretching in neat lines on each side, like rulings on the two pages of an exercise book, one each side of the central fold, with hassocks like little blobs of red ink here and there. He would be no bigger than a black beetle, and so far away that his grumblings and snufflings would be lost in mid-air long before they reached the vasty heights where the lone Paul-bird hovered unseen.

He would swoop next, down and down, to lift Mrs Curdle's painted roof. Paul thrilled at the thought of it. He would touch it very gently, he told himself, for it was as old as it was beautiful, and as awe-inspiring as it was gay. Molly had told him all about Mrs Curdle and gipsies' ways. She would be standing by her glittering stove, cooking hedgehogs, Paul had no doubt. He had once, fearfully, climbed the three steps to Mrs Curdle's caravan and had gazed, fascinated, at the glory within, the half-door had been shut, but by standing on tip-toe he had seen the shelves, the tiny drawers, the cupboards, the gleaming brass and copper, and the rows of vivid painted plates as breath-takingly lovely to the child as the bright birds which he had seen the week before at the Zoo, sitting motionless upon their perches, in a splendour of tropical plumage.

No one had been in the caravan. Only a clock ticked and a saucepan sizzled, now and then, upon the diminutive stove. Molly had stood beside him and had pointed out one particularly small drawer close by the door. It had a curious brass handle, embossed with leaves and fruit.

'She puts the money in there,' had whispered Molly, in the child's ear.

'What money?' Paul had asked.

'The fortune-telling money. See, she leans over this door and reads your palm and you pays her a bit of silver, six-pence say, or a shilling, and she pops it in this little drawer just beside her. Real handy, isn't it, Paul?'

He had nodded, open-mouthed, and would have liked to have stayed longer, just gazing at the beauties, but Molly had hurried him away.

'And would we have seen a sixpence or a shilling if we'd opened that little drawer?' he had asked her later, as she bathed him.

Molly's eyes had grown as round as an owl's.

'It would have been *stuffed tight* with silver. And gold sovereigns too, most like. And too heavy to move, ten to one.'

Paul had been most impressed, so that now, on his astral travels he looked at the interior of Mrs Curdle's caravan with the eye of reverence. There would be so many things to see that it would be hard to distinguish separate objects. It would be like looking into his own toy kaleidoscope, a glory of shifting colour, winking lights, shimmering reflections, and endless enchanting patterns.

Would Mrs Curdle be there at nearly ten-thirty in the morning? Paul shivered at the thought of seeing her, even if he himself could remain invisible, for Molly had told him that gipsies could cast spells, just as witches did.

She might, thought Paul, pleasurably apprehensive, be making a little clay doll to stick with pins, so that the real person it was meant to be would suffer pains. Supposing she *knew* he was watching without having to look up? Sup-posing the doll was meant to be Paul Young?

The crick in his neck came back unaccountably and Paul

threw away his idea of being a giant bird. It wasn't as good as he'd first thought.

He ran to the door and opened it, suddenly in need of company.

The smell of coffee brewing floated from downstairs and the sound of Aunt Ruth singing happily to herself as she clack-clacked across the stone-flagged kitchen in her high-heeled sandals.

'Aunt Ruth, Aunt Ruth!' he called urgently. 'Come and watch me stand on my head!'

The sense of mercies received, to which Ruth had woken that morning, remained with her as she worked about the house. She was astonished at this new inner peace, bewildered but grateful for the strength which had ebbed back to her. It was as though some throbbing wound had miraculously healed overnight and the scab which had formed over it could be touched without dread. For the first time Ruth found that she could recall the whole tragic affair dispassionately.

She had become engaged to Stephen Gardiner just over a year ago amidst general approval. Only her father had looked coolly at the young man and had remained un-affected by the fair good looks and charming boyish manner which won Stephen so many friends. He was employed in a firm of tea and coffee importers and went daily by Tube train to the City. His income was comfortable enough to support a young wife, his health was excellent, his family background very similar to that of the Bassetts, and he was head over heels in love with his pretty Ruth and there was no reason for her father to refuse his consent. Nor did he. But he could not whole-heartedly like this young man. For some reason Stephen's straight blue gaze, his deferential manner, and his ease with the ladies of the Bassett household aroused a small, nagging distrust in Mr Bassett's heart, and Ruth was aware of it. She had taxed him once when they were alone together.

'What is it that you dislike in Stephen?' Her father had answered her honestly.

'I don't know, my dear, I just don't know. If he's your choice, I'm content to abide by it. But one thing I would like to ask you.'

'And what's that?' she had answered.

'Don't marry too soon. Stephen tells me you'd like to marry this summer. Well, don't, my dear. Leave it until next spring, and I shall feel a lot happier.'

She had smiled and told him that she would talk to Stephen about it.

'We don't want to see you go, you know,' her father had said, smiling back at her.

And so the wedding had been fixed for the first week in March, and the young couple had planned to go away for their honeymoon in Italy just before Easter.

Early in the year they had found a flat in Kensington. It was the top floor of a Victorian house, in a quiet leafy road, shabby, but comfortable, with big rooms and broad windows. It would be convenient for Stephen's journey to the City and for Ruth's office job in Ealing which she proposed to continue after marriage. They spent their evenings painting walls, choosing curtains, planning their furnishings, and dreaming of the future. Ruth never for one moment had any doubts about their happiness together. She moved towards her wedding day with serenity, unmoved by the bustle of activity accompanying her. Her mother's complicated plans for the wedding breakfast, the invitations, the presents, the cake, the organist, the bell-ringers, the bridesmaids, the trousseau, and all the other paraphernalia of a suitable wedding left her unperturbed. All would be well, she knew. Nothing could alter the unshakeable fact that she and Stephen would be married and living together in the adorable flat before the end of March.

Looking back on that halcyon period, after the blow, Ruth became aware of numberless small things which should have warned her of Stephen's waning affections. He was a man who was accustomed to success in every undertaking. He approached his goals directly and with ease, and the long engagement was particularly frustrating to one of his impatient and ambitious calibre. Would all have been well, Ruth sometimes wondered, if they had married earlier, or, as her father had suspected, would Stephen's deflection have occurred in any case, and then had more serious consequences? It was one of those unanswerable problems which were to torture poor Ruth for many sad weeks.

But at the time only one small incident had ruffled her calm. Stephen had been offered a position in the firm which made it necessary to take charge of their office in Brazil for two or perhaps three years. He had told her this news one rainy spring evening as they sat on the floor of the empty dining-room at the flat, painting the skirting board. Ruth had not even bothered to look up from her work.

'It's out of the question, of course,' she had said, drawing her brush carefully along the wood.

'It's promotion, and we could do with it,' Stephen had answered, so shortly, that she had put down her brush and gazed at him. His cheek twitched with a tense muscle and she realized, with a sharp stabbing pain, that he had looked strained and tired for some time. She spoke gently.

'If you honestly think we should –' she had begun.

'What's there to stay for?' he had answered.

'Why, this!' she had responded, waving her hand at the new paint around them.

'Four frowsty rooms in a scruffy little backwater,' he had

scoffed. ' "Caged in Kensington." What a title for a domestic tragedy!'

Perplexed and hurt, Ruth had tried to answer him. She had told him that if he felt like that then they would certainly go to Brazil together. She made him promise to see his doctor about the headaches that had been plaguing him. She was positive that he needed glasses. That direct, intense gaze, which fluttered so many hearts, might well be due to short sight and nothing more glamorous, but he had a great aversion to wearing spectacles and brushed away her suggestions of a visit to the oculist.

Later, he had comforted her, called himself a brute, a selfish pig, promised her that all would be well when they were married, and had begged her to forget all about Brazil. They would be far better off as they were for the first year or two of their married life, and other opportunities would crop up he knew.

But Ruth was not entirely comforted, and although she seemed as tranquil as before, she watched Stephen secretly, conscious that he was working long hours under strain. But it was a transitory malaise, she felt certain, which would pass away as soon as they were married.

One morning, four days before the wedding, Ruth's dress arrived, a misty white armful of chiffon and lace, which emerged from a cocoon of rustling tissue paper. The post had arrived at the same time and her father sat at the breakfast table, gazing fixedly at a short note written in Stephen Gardiner's hand. He rose from the table and looked across at his daughter and his wife.

Ruth was pirouetting about the room, the fragile frock swirling as she held it against her. Mrs Bassett's face was alight with wonderment.

'My dear,' said Mr Bassett, in a husky voice, 'leave that

child to her own devices for a minute and come and help me on with my coat.'

The two went into the hall and Mr Bassett closed the door. Then he handed the note to his wife. Her face crumpled as she read, but she made no sound. The letter bore the address of a Swiss hotel and began without preamble.

I've made a hopeless mess of everything. Tell Ruth it's no use going on with the wedding and better to part now. She'll get a letter by the next post, but tell her not to think too badly of me. She's always been too good for me in any case. Forgive me if you can.

Stephen

'He's ill. He's not himself,' whispered Mrs Bassett at last, raising tear-filled eyes. Her husband looked grim.

'I'll try and book an air passage today,' said Mr Bassett, 'to see the fellow.'

'And Ruth?' faltered his wife.

'Break it to her before the afternoon post arrives,' answered Mr Bassett, transferring the burden with customary male ability. 'You'll do it better than I can. I'll see her when I get back.'

He kissed his wife swiftly, crammed the letter in his pocket, and escaped through the front door.

Ruth had received the news later that morning with amazing tranquillity. Her reaction had been the same as her mother's. Stephen was not himself. This sudden flight, the agitated note, the panic before the ceremony, were all symptoms of intolerable strain. The appalling thought that Stephen might really leave her and that the wedding might never take place hardly entered her head. The plans were made, the guests invited, the beds in the house were already made up awaiting elderly aunts from Cheltenham, a Scottish cousin, and a school friend from Holland. The wedding was as inevitable to Ruth as the approach of dawn, and though her heart was wrung with pity for Stephen, she felt none for herself. There was no need.

It was she who calmed her mother that day. She read her letter from Stephen, which arrived that afternoon, in her bedroom, with the white wedding dress at her side. It added little more to the one her father had received, except that the post in Brazil was mentioned. He urged her to forget him, to forgive him, to waste no time in regrets. Better by far to part now, was the gist of the distracted communication, than to find out their mistake too late.

Ruth felt that she should go at once to Switzerland to see Stephen, but her mother insisted that she should await her father's return the next day. Both women slept little that night. Mrs Bassett knew instinctively that Stephen would never be persuaded to return. Besides her grief on Ruth's account her racked mind agitated itself with plans for the cancellation of the ceremony. At three o'clock she rose and paced distractedly about the quiet house, and Ruth joined her, equally distraught, but not for herself. She grieved for her unhappy lover, her agitated mother, and her father's journeyings. She longed for his return which she was positive would bring good news, and possibly Stephen himself.

And so the blow for Ruth was all the more annihilating. When her father returned, grey-faced and weary, to tell her that there was no hope at all of a reconciliation, that Stephen had already accepted the post in Brazil and was to fly out on the day that was to have been his wedding day, and that he never wished to see Ruth again, the girl collapsed. Even then the tears refused to come. She lay in bed, white and small, dark eyes roving restlessly about her room, unable to eat or speak, while the dreadful news was dispatched to the invited guests, friends, neighbours, caterers, and all.

When she was fit to travel her father had driven her down to stay with her sister Joan, still numb with shock, a woe-begone little ghost. And there, throughout the slowly unfolding spring, amid the kindly scents and sounds of Thrush Green, her frozen heart thawed again.

The sound of her nephew calling from upstairs roused Ruth from her musings. She left the coffee brewing and ran upstairs to see the little boy, pausing at the landing window to look at the golden glory outside.

The horse chestnut trees were beginning to break, their palmate leaves looking like tiny green hands bursting from sticky brown gloves. She could see the children running about in the playground, their hair flying in the wind, their arms and legs gleaming like satin in the morning sunshine.

Miss Bembridge was coming from Doctor Bailey's house and Ruth watched her sturdy figure stump along the road to the cottage on the corner. The surgery door opened again and young Doctor Lovell stood for a moment upon the threshold, before setting off across Thrush Green. Ruth watched his advancing figure with growing comfort.

'Paul!' she called, hurrying across to the bedroom. 'Doctor's coming!'

Paul was scrambling into his tousled bed as she opened his door. He looked up at her, open-mouthed.

'Aunt Ruth,' he said in astonishment, 'your eyes are shining.'

6. Coffee at The Fuchsia Bush

MRS BAILEY was enjoying a cup of coffee in The Fuchsia Bush, Lulling's rendezvous for the ladies of that small town. She had left the doctor in the garden, happily slicing the edges of the flower beds with a formidably sharp new edge-cutter, and more full of zest than she had seen him for many weeks.

She had tripped lightfoot down from Thrush Green, rejoicing in the sparkling morning and the exhilarating sounds of the fair's preparations. But now, with the shopping safely in her basket, she was quite pleased to sit alone, watching the inhabitants of Lulling pass by on their lawful occasions, before facing the long uphill pull to her house.

The Fuchsia Bush prided itself on its appearance. Its architect had done his best to make a building which would harmonize with the surrounding Cotswold stone and yet suggest the 'cosy-chintzes-within' atmosphere which his clients had insisted upon. An enormous bow window with several of its panes devoted to a bottle-glass effect, kept his clients happy, and later their customers, for it was generally accepted in Lulling that the appearance of one's friends gazing through the bottle-glass panes was a never-to-be-forgotten experience. Like gigantic carp they goggled and gulped and when embellished with hats, or, better still, spectacles, even the handsomest of Lulling's inhabitants could strike fear and awe into the beholder's marrow.

Mrs Bailey stirred her coffee slowly and read the new placard outside the chapel opposite. It said:

THE WAGES OF SIN IS DEATH

which Mrs Bailey found more grammatically irritating than thought-provoking. She suddenly remembered that, years ago, she had heard of a firm that had written across its delivery van:

MAYS WAYS PAYS ALWAYS

'And at least', thought Mrs Bailey, snatching comfort where she could, 'I was never forced to see that!' She turned her attention to the interior of The Fuchsia Bush.

Apart from two elderly men in mufflers, who sipped their coffee noisily and discussed chess, Mrs Bailey was the only customer. Two girls, in mauve overalls with cherry-coloured cuffs and collars, did their best to emulate fuchsia flowers, and certainly drooped silently against the grey walls quite successfully. A stack of mauve- and cherry-striped boxes stood on the glass counter in readiness to hold the excellent home-made cakes which were already cooling in the window, adding their fragrance to that of the coffee. A beam of sunlight fell suddenly upon Mrs Bailey's hand, the first real warmth for months, she thought delightedly, and her spirits rose at this token of the summer to come.

What fun Lulling was, she told herself for the thousandth time! She looked affectionately at the old men, the lackadaisical waitresses, the chapel notice, the leisurely moving few people walking outside on the wide pavement beneath the whispering lime trees. I suppose I'm so fond of it because I'm really part of it, she mused to herself. 'Attached to it,' she added, echoing Eeyore as he mourned his lost tail; for Mrs Bailey's mind was a rag-bag of snippets, some of which she drew out for herself to admire and delight in, and some of which fell out of their own accord, gay unconsidered trifles which she had long forgotten, as in the present case, but which afforded her infinite joy when they reappeared.

The door swung open and interrupted Mrs Bailey's ponderings. Ella Bembridge blew in, her felt hat jammed low over her brow, followed by Dimity Dean bearing a laden basket. The room, which had seemed so large and peaceful, suddenly shrank to half its size and became a battleground of conflicting noises as Ella Bembridge thrust her way between wheel-backed chairs, booming cheerful greetings. It was at times like this that Mrs Bailey had the feeling that she had at last grasped Einstein's theory of relativity, but it was always a fleeting glimpse of Olympian clarity, and almost at once the clouds would close over that bright vision and Mrs Bailey would realize that she was still in her usual woolly-minded world of three dimensions.

'Anyone with you? Coming, I mean?' shouted Ella.

'No. No one,' responded Mrs Bailey, lifting her basket from a chair and smiling at Dimity who collapsed upon it gratefully.

'Just been to get –' began Dimity in an exhausted whisper.

'My prescription made up,' roared Ella.

'The fish,' added Dimity.

'For my rash,' boomed Ella.

'For lunch,' finished Dimity.

Mrs Bailey was quite used to this dual form of conversation and nodded politely.

'Think that young Lovell knows what's he's up to?' asked Ella, planting her sturdy brogues well apart and affording the assembled company an unlovely view of the formidable underclothes which had offended Doctor Lovell earlier that morning.

'I'm sure he does,' answered Mrs Bailey equably. She wondered how many more questions Ella would ask.

'How's your husband? Taking a partner yet?' went on Miss Bembridge, feeling in her jacket pocket.

'Much better,' said Mrs. Bailey, answering the first, and

ignoring the second question. Ella produced a worn tobacco
tin, undid it, took out a cigarette paper from a small folder,
pinched up a vicious-looking dollop of black tobacco from
the depths of the tin, and began to roll a very untidy cigarette.

'Oh, do let me do it for you, darling,' said Miss Dean,
leaning forward eagerly.

'Don't fuss so, Dim,' said her friend brusquely, raising the
limp tube to her mouth and licking the edge of the paper
with a thick wet tongue. She lit the straggling tobacco
which cascaded from one end, inhaled strongly, and blew
two terrifying blasts down her nostrils. Mrs Bailey was
reminded of the rocking-horse which had lived in her
nursery sixty years earlier, and would have liked the
leisure to recall its half-forgotten beauties, the dappled
flanks, the scarlet harness bright with gilded studs, and its
worn hospitable saddle. But no one mused in Ella's
company.

'Hell of a time that girl takes getting the coffee,' said she,
in far too carrying a voice for Mrs Bailey's peace of mind.
One of the drooping fuchsias detached herself from the wall
and drifted towards the kitchen.

'We oughtn't to be too long –' began Dimity timidly,
hauling up a watch on a long silver chain from the recesses
of her bodice.

'Doesn't matter if we fry it!' responded her friend. Dimity looked tearful.

'But you know it doesn't –'

'Agree with me?' boomed Miss Bembridge menacingly.
'Of course it does! Fried fish is the only way to eat the
stuff.'

'But the doctor said only this morning that you shouldn't
touch fried food, darling, with that rash. It's for your
own –'

Ella broke in mercilessly, tapping her cigarette ash force-fully into Mrs Bailey's saucer.

'My own good! I know, I know! Well, I've said we'll have it in parsley sauce, much as I detest it, so let's forget it.'

Dimity turned apologetically to Mrs Bailey.

'I do feel fish is so much more wholesome in a mild white sauce. So pure and nourishing, and so light too. But it takes longer to cook of course. I said to Ella this morning, "A little light fish, or perhaps a boiled egg, while you've got that rash, will be the most *wholesome* thing you can have." '

Mrs Bailey smiled and nodded and thought of Mr Wood-house, her favourite Emma's father, who also recommended boiled eggs. 'An egg boiled very soft is not unwholesome. Mrs Bates, let me propose your venturing on one of these eggs.' And she wondered, looking at Dimity's pathetic anxiety, if she might be driven by it to go even further and suggest 'a small basin of thin gruel', which was all that Mr Woodhouse could honestly recommend, if Miss Bem-bridge's rash persisted. For the sake of the friends' domestic harmony Mrs Bailey prayed that Doctor Lovell's prescrip-tion would be speedily successful.

It was at this moment that Dotty Harmer fumbled her way into The Fuchsia Bush. Her steel spectacles were awry, her woollen stockings lay, as always, in wrinkles round her chicken-thin legs, and her hair sprouted at all angles beneath a speckled grey chip-straw hat.

The less languid of the attendants went forward to greet her.

'Just one of your small stone-milled loaves, please,' mur-mured Dotty, peering into the glass cabinet that held the loaves.

The girl replied with considerable satisfaction, that all the small ones had been sold, but there was most providentially, just one large one left. This threw Dotty into the greatest agitation. She dumped her string bag on the floor, thrust her hat farther back upon her head, and began to pour out her troubles.

'But I can't possibly use a large loaf! Living alone as I do a small one lasts me three days at least, and even if I make rusks of the last bit for the animals it is really more than I can manage. And in any case, now that the weather has turned warm I shan't need to light the stove and so there will be no means of making the rusks!'

The girl suggested a small white loaf. Dotty's agitation was now tinged with horror.

'A *white* loaf?' squeaked Dotty, with such repugnance, that one might reasonably have supposed that she had been offered bread made from fine-ground human bones. 'You should know by now my feelings about *white* bread. It never, never appears in my house!'

'*Dotty!*' bawled Miss Bembridge, at this point, in a voice that set the crockery rattling. 'Get them to cut it in half!'

The girl cast Ella a look so deadly that it was a wonder that Miss Bembridge's ample form was not shrivelled to a small dead leaf. Dotty's face, however, was alight with relief.

'Dear Ella! How sensible! Yes, of course,' she said, turning to the assistant, 'just cut the large wholemeal one in half.'

The girl flounced off to the kitchen, lips compressed, and returned with a bread board and knife. She cut the loaf in two and held the board out for Dotty's inspection.

'Oh, dear,' said Dotty, her face clouding again, 'I wonder if I really need half. It's quite a large amount, isn't it? I mean, for one person?' She peered anxiously at the girl's face for some help, but received none.

After some tut-tutting she lifted first one piece of bread

to the light, and then the other. She then sniffed at each, tasted a crumb or two which had fallen on to the board, and began to shake her head doubtfully.

Mrs Bailey became conscious that the bread knife still remained within the grip of the silent waitress, and felt that the time had come to intervene.

'There are always the birds, Dotty dear,' she pointed out. 'Take the crustier half and come and have coffee.'

Dotty nodded and smiled. The girl flung one half into a paper bag and handed the bread board to her colleague with a long-suffering look. The knife, Mrs Bailey was relieved to see, she set aside on a shelf, while she stood watching Dotty fumble among a dozen compartments of a large black purse for the money. Dotty's fingers, stained with many a herb, scrabbled first here, then there, and the girl's foot began to tap ominously on the shining linoleum.

As last Dotty raised a damp worried gaze from her labours and said:

'I appear to have only a coat button, my door key, and an Irish sixpence. Unless,' she added, drawing forth a very crumpled piece of paper, 'you can change a five-pound note!'

Ben Curdle, stripped to the waist in the morning sunshine, sat on the grass with his back propped against one wheel of his caravan and a bottle of beer from The Two Pheasants propped between his knees.

He had been hard at work now for over four hours. The main stands were all erected and Ben had just finished helping his cousin, Sam, to hitch the swing-boats into place. It was heavy work, for the boats were old and cumbersome though they looked gay enough, he admitted, with the fresh paint they had put on during the winter. If he had his way, thought Ben, he'd scrap them and get some of those new light ones. Just as safe and not so back-breaking to heave about. But with Gran as she was, what was the good of suggesting it?

He watched his cousin Sam who was sitting on the steps of his caravan with his flashy young wife. Ben had never liked either of them. He'd never trusted Sam since he had found him boasting one day of some shirts which he had stolen from a line in some cottage garden. It was not the sort of thing the Curdles did. If his old Gran had ever heard about it Sam would have been given his marching orders, Ben knew. The incident had occurred many years before and Ben had made it pretty plain just what he thought of such goings-on, putting up with the tauntings of the older man in dour silence.

A few months later Sam had married. Mrs Curdle did not approve of the match. The girl, she told Sam bluntly, 'had been anyone's' in the small Thames-side town from which he had brought her, but providing she buckled-to and worked her way with the fair old Mrs Curdle was agreeable to her joining them. The girl, Bella, had had the sense to keep out of the old lady's way as far as was possible, but she deeply resented the matriarch's caustic remarks about her thatch of hair, as yellow and brittle as straw from frequent dousings with peroxide, and the comments on her wardrobe to which she gave considerable thought and expenditure. Sam bore the brunt of his wife's resentment in the privacy of their small caravan, and he often thought sadly to himself that although she was a real smart bit her tongue could fair flay a man. Three children had been born to them, whining and wet-nosed, but all three dressed extravagantly in the bright and shiny satins to which their mother was addicted.

Ben watched the family now, and wondered, not for the first time, just how Sam managed to dress all that lot. There was fat old Bella in that red frock – a new one bought in the last town, he knew. And she had flaunted a watch under his nose last week that she'd told him Sam had bought for her. She'd said he'd been lucky with the horses, but you didn't have to be a wizard to know that horses let you down more often than they came home, mused young Ben.

He drained his bottle, wiped his mouth on the back of his hand, and leant forward upon the warm comfort of his knees under their black corduroy covering. He felt pretty sure that Sam was getting money dishonestly, and he could guess where. He knew, as did all the great Curdle family, exactly how much each of them received each week, for on Friday night the ritual of paying out took place.

The heads of each family and the single members, such as Ben, who were still under age and under Mrs Curdle's direct protection, assembled in the old lady's caravan as soon as the lights of the fair had gone out. All the money from that night's stand was put into a great brass bowl ready to be transferred to a battered attaché case which was kept at the foot of Mrs Curdle's mattress and was the Curdle Bank. Meanwhile the old lady had counted the week's takings already in the case and had allotted them with scrupulous justice to all concerned. Those with children had more, naturally, than those without. Mrs Curdle would tell the company how much had been earned and would then call out each name in turn. The piles of money stood stacked before her on a small card-table, which she had used to support her crystal in earlier days. The wages varied, of course, from week to week, according to the size of the town which the fair was visiting, the weather, rival attractions, accidents to gear, and so on. But each man knew that the fierce old lady whose hawk-gaze terrified him was absolutely, ferociously, searingly honest, and if the handful

of coins was pitifully small, as sometimes it was, without
any doubt he had his right and proper share.

There had been one or two members of the family who
had demurred at this despotism in their time. They had
been given their choice – to go or to stay willingly. Two
had gone, and no one had ever heard of their fortunes, nor
had Mrs Curdle made any inquiries about them. They had
left the Curdle family, therefore Mrs Curdle had no further
interest in them. The others elected to stay, and they spoke
no more heresy.

There were two ways, Ben knew, in which Sam could
help himself to money. In the first place he could secrete
some from his own takings and pay in the rest after each
day's work. This was not as easy as it seemed, for many eyes
were about, the helpers on his stand would soon become
suspicious, and, in any case, the old lady, after years of
experience, had a fairly shrewd idea of the amount to be
expected.

There was a second way. Mrs Curdle had become increasingly careless of late in the disposal of the money. She
was ill, she was old, she was habitually tired, and to heave
up the mattress to put away odd sums of money in the case
was becoming a burden. Quite often, Ben knew, she thrust
it into the little drawer by the side of the half-door, or into
a pewter tea-pot which stood on the mantelpiece beside the
photograph of his dead father. Usually she roused herself
to transfer it to the case, but Ben had seen, only the week
before, notes and silver stuffed into the narrow dresser
drawer, which hitherto had only held a shilling or two for a
passing beggar or for the purchase of a loaf or a bottle of
milk from some travelling tradesman that the caravans
might meet in the lanes.

The family came and went to its head's caravan a dozen
times a day, and it would be the easiest thing in the world

to abstract money from the drawer in Mrs Curdle's absence. Sam made bets almost daily, and lately they had been heavier, Ben knew.

St Andrew's Church chimed the half-hour and Ben stirred himself. Half past eleven already! He leapt to his feet, stretching his arms luxuriously above his head. His corduroy trousers slipped, cool and comfortable, round his bare waist and the light breeze played across his naked shoulders refreshingly.

He thought, with sudden joy, of his Molly. By half past one he hoped to see her again. As soon as he had had his dinner with Gran, he would set off alone, through Lulling Woods to The Drovers' Arms. She would be in the bar then, and with any luck would be free from two o'clock. He could hardly believe his good fortune in finding her again.

He became conscious that Sam was calling to him to give a hand with the bell-tent which housed the small menagerie. Another hour's hard work would see the fair ready and waiting for the evening's fun. And then, Ben told himself, he had two more jobs ahead. To find Molly – that was the first and all-important one; and to keep a sharp eye on the movements of his cousin Sam to confirm his suspicions.

'Coming, Sam!' he called, and went methodically about the first of the tasks ahead.

After coffee the four ladies had returned together up the hill from Lulling. It was soon after twelve as they stood making their farewells on the corner of Thrush Green near the church. The sun was now overhead in a cloudless sky of powdery blue. The rooks were wheeling above the clump of elm trees by the path which led to Dotty Harmer's cottage, the dew had vanished from the grass, and the shadows of the trees in the horse-chestnut avenue lay fore-shortened, like dark pools, at the foot of the trunks. Later they would creep, longer and longer, across the grass until they almost reached the edge of the green opposite Doctor Bailey's house, and then, Mrs Bailey knew from many years' experience, that meant that it was almost time for the music of the fair to begin.

The heat shimmered above the caravans and along the white road to Nod and Nidden. The school-children were skipping and darting home to their dinners.

Dotty Harmer, her half-loaf clutched against her chest and the bulging string bag dangling at her side, was the first to leave the group and vanish down the narrow passage between the Piggotts' cottage and The Two Pheasants.

'And I wonder what *her* lunch is!' said Miss Bembridge. 'Fried frogs with dandelion sauce, I expect. Poor old Dotty!'

The mention of lunch threw Dimity Dean into extreme agitation.

'We simply *must* fly,' she said to Mrs Bailey. Her watery eyes, screwed up against the sunshine, turned to St Andrew's clock, which gave her small comfort.

'Darling,' she squeaked, in horror. 'Look, ten past twelve and the fish still to be done!' She tugged ineffectually at Ella Bembridge's bolster-like arm. So might a fluttering fledgling have attempted to pull off a branch.

Miss Bembridge gave a sigh that rustled the tissue paper over the lettuce in Mrs Bailey's basket.

'Needs must, I suppose, when the devil drives!' she boomed, and the two friends set off to their cottage leaving Mrs Bailey to cross the grass to her own home.

A piquant smell of fried pork chops and onions wafted from Mrs Curdle's caravan as the doctor's wife passed nearby. The old lady was preparing lunch for herself and for Ben. Mrs Bailey thought wryly of the bouquet which no doubt already lay in the matriarch's home, awaiting its bestowal, and she remembered, with a pang, that this might well be the last time that she would smell Mrs Curdle's mid-day meal and receive a bunch of flowers, garish and gaudy but made with love and in a spirit of steadfast gratitude, from those gnarled dusky hands.

Mrs Bailey paused with her hand on her gate and looked back at the morning glory of Thrush Green. Would it ever look like this again on the first day of May, so blue, so golden, so breathtakingly innocent?

She looked with affection at the cheerful bustle of the little fairground, the tents, the flapping canvas, the blue smoke spiralling from a camp fire, and the brightly clad fair folk moving among it all. They were as gay as butterflies, thought Mrs Bailey, and as ephemeral. By tomorrow the fair would be over, and only a ring of cold ashes and the ruts made by wooden wheels would remind them of their visitors. The mellow enduring houses, which sat like sun-ning cats, four-square and tranquil, around the wide expanse of Thrush Green would have it to themselves again after tonight's brief bonfire-blaze of glory.

'A pity!' said Mrs Bailey, with a sigh, looking across at Mrs Curdle's caravan, blooming like some gay transient flower against the grey background of St Andrew's. 'We've weathered a lot together.'

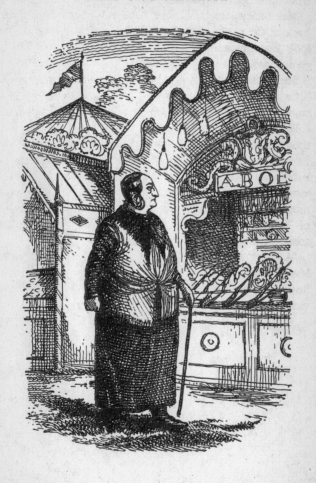

7. Noonday Heat

THRUSH GREEN drowsed under the growing heat of the midday sun. It was that somnolent time, soon after one o'clock, when everything lay hushed. In cottage kitchens, where the midday dinner had been served an hour before, the plates had been washed and returned to their shelves, the tables had been scrubbed, the checked cloths spread upon them, and the potted plants placed to the best advantage. After the hubbub of the morning the kitchens showed their peaceful afternoon faces, while their owners dozed in the armchairs by the hob or settled down to enjoy a quiet cup of tea.

The steady ticking of a clock, the sizzle of a kettle, or the rustle of a slowly read newspaper were the only sounds to be heard in that tranquil haven of time between the two tides of morning and afternoon.

But in the big sunny kitchen at the Bassets' Ruth and Paul had only just finished their meal. Much to Paul's joy Doctor Lovell had said that he could get up, and providing that he had an hour's rest later in the day he could go to the fair for a short while.

'And you'll be fit for school on Monday,' he had pronounced. Paul, young enough still to dote on this institution, was energetic in his thanks.

He had eaten well, demolishing a plate of cherries, bottled earlier by his mother, and now rattled on gaily as he counted his stones.

Ruth sat beside him still in a state of bemusement at the inner peace which now engulfed her. Her gaze was fixed upon the sunlit garden, and she hardly heard the little boy.

'Mummy says girls count their stones to see who they'll marry, and boys count to see what they'll be,' chattered Paul busily. 'So I'll tell you what I'm going to be.'

He counted slowly, nodding his way through the rhyme:

> 'Tinker, tailor, soldier, sailor,
> Rich man, poor man, beggar man, thief,
> Tinker, tailor –'

He paused and sighed heavily.

'A tailor, Aunt Ruth! Hear that? A tailor! I wouldn't want to be a *tailor*, would you?'

Ruth roused herself.

'I'll tell you another rhyme,' she said, taking the spoon from her nephew. She leant over the plate and recited slowly:

> 'Soldier bold, sailor true,
> Skilled physician, Cambridge blue,
> Titled noble, squire hale,
> Portly rector, curate pale.
> Soldier bold, sailor true –'

'How's that?' she inquired, looking at him.

'Sailor true,' Paul nodded with immense satisfaction. 'Much better. I'd like that!'

Ruth put down the spoon and was about to collect the plates but Paul stopped her.

'Your turn, Aunt Ruth. I'll see who you're going to marry. Say it with me.'

Together they chanted slowly, pushing the wine-coloured stones along the rim of the blue and white plates.

> 'Soldier bold, sailor true,
> Skilled physician, Cambridge blue,
> Titled noble, squire hale,

Portly rector, curate pale,
Soldier bold, sailor true,
Skilled physician –'

Ruth put down the spoon hastily as she came to the last of the stones.

'What's that?' inquired Paul.

'A doctor,' said Ruth, brushing the stones into one plate.

'Like Doctor Lovell?' asked the child.

'Or Doctor Bailey,' said Ruth evenly. She rose and took the plates to the sink.

'He's too old,' objected Paul, 'and Mrs Bailey might not want you. But Doctor Lovell would do.'

'If I'd had one less cherry, Paul, I might have married you,' said Ruth, smiling at him. But the child was not to be put off his train of thought so easily, Ruth noticed wryly.

'Doctor Lovell's very nice,' persisted the child. 'Would you marry him?'

'Of course not!'

'Why not?'

'For one thing he hasn't asked me,' Ruth said lightly. 'Now, would you like to play in the garden while I wash up?'

The child ignored this suggestion and fixed his remorseless blue gaze upon his aunt. Ruth could not help feeling like a mother bird who has trailed a wing before some particularly dogged hunter only to find her wiles are of no avail.

'But if he *did*!' insisted Paul, clinging to the side of the sink, and staring unblinkingly at his victim. 'The stones *said* a skilled fizzun and that probably means Doctor Lovell. And he is a real *nice* man. You *ought* to marry him if the stones say you ought. It's what –'

Ruth cut him short impatiently.

'Oh, don't fuss so, Paul! It's only a rhyme and doesn't mean a thing. Out you go now, while I wash up.'

The boy disengaged himself slowly. It was obvious that his thoughts were wholly of the signs and portents of the cherry stones, but, child-like, he turned the situation to his own advantage.

'Can I go and see Bobby Anderson, before he goes into school?'

Ruth hesitated. She did not like the child to roam Thrush Green unaccompanied, but he could not come to much harm if he were within sight of the house, and she felt the need of a few minutes' solitude to collect her wits. The child, watching her, guessed her thoughts, but felt that all would fall out as he wished.

'Just for a little while then. But come back when the school bell goes at a quarter to two.'

'Can I show him the postcard Mummy sent?' This was a fascinating picture of a cat with large glass eyes which rolled about in the most enchanting manner, and had given the bed-bound Paul immense joy.

'Of course you can,' said his aunt. 'But put on your linen hat, and don't forget to keep in sight of the house. I may want you before a quarter to two.'

The child rushed from the kitchen and Ruth heard him bounding up the stairs in search of his postcard.

'And let's hope it puts other ideas out of his head,' muttered his aunt aloud. But, as she disposed of the cherry stones which had caused so much discussion, she could not help but notice that the 'other ideas' continued to flicker and dance in her own mind like the warm sunbeams that sparkled and twinkled about her as she splashed water into the bowl.

Paul, clutching his postcard and crowned, obediently, with his linen hat, ran down the path to the green outside.

The hush which enveloped Thrush Green threw its spell over the excited little boy and his pace slowed as soon as he emerged from his own garden. There was no breeze now. The bright caravans, the trees, the daisy-spangled grass of Thrush Green lay, like a painted back-cloth, motionless and unreal. It was an enchanted world, doubly arresting to the child who had been housebound for several days.

He looked, with new wonder, at the blossoming cherry tree, which overhung the low stone wall of the next-door garden. For the first time he noticed, with a thrill of joy, the delicate white flowers suspended by thread-like stalks to the black tracery of the boughs. Those threads, he realized suddenly, would dangle cherries later where the flowers now danced, and he would be able to hang them over his ears and waggle his head gently from side to side for the pleasure of feeling the firm glossy berries nudging his cheek. It was a moment of poignant discovery for young Paul, and he felt a thrill of pride as he realized that he knew now exactly how the cherries came to be. In future they would be doubly beautiful, for he would remember the glory of that pendant snow even as he sensuously enjoyed the feel of the fruit against his face and the cool freshness in his mouth as he bit it.

He found Bobby Anderson lying on his stomach, a daisy stalk between his lips and legs waving idly, for even this vociferous youngster had succumbed to the spell of mid-day sloth.

'Smashing!' was his verdict on the treasured postcard.

Paul glowed in the sunshine of his hero's approbation.

'You comin' in then?' asked Bobby, nodding towards the school.

'Monday, not now,' answered Paul casually. It was won-derful to be able to dismiss school so airily.

'Bet you've been sucking up to ol' Doctor Whatsit,' grumbled Bobby enviously. Paul was stung.

'No, I didn't then,' he protested indignantly, 'but I've got to have a rest this afternoon.'

Bobby Anderson contorted his features into a hideous travesty of a crying baby.

' "Got to have a rest," ' he mimicked, in a maddening, mewing squeak. 'You and your rest!' he continued, in normal tones of extreme scorn. 'In your soppy ol' hat!' he added, tipping it off with an adroit blow.

Paul was about to join battle inflamed by this last insult, but Miss Watson appeared in the school doorway, and instantly, Bobby fled to her across the playground, crying urgently as he went:

'Can I ring the bell, miss? Miss, miss, please let me!'

Paul watched his friend and tormentor vanish into the porch. Two seconds later the bell above the steep-pitched roof gave out its cracked message, and Paul knew that Bobby's sturdy frame was swinging lustily on the end of the bell-rope hidden within.

Nearly a quarter to two already, and he hadn't done half the things he had intended, thought Paul mournfully. He turned his back upon the school and looked, with some awe, upon Mrs Curdle's distant caravan. As he watched, he saw the old lady emerge, carrying a bucket. There was an arc of flashing water as she tossed its contents into the sunshine, and then she stood motionless, a massive, majestic figure against the dazzling sky.

Paul saw that she was watching somebody who was crossing the grass towards him. As the figure approached him Paul recognized it joyfully. It was Ben – his Molly's Ben – and he was waving to him!

'How do, Paul?' asked the young man, smiling down at the little boy.

'Very well, thank you,' responded Paul, flushing at this unexpected honour.

'Bet you don't remember me,' said Ben. His voice held a slight query and he seemed unaccountably anxious. Paul hastily reassured him.

' 'Course I do. You're Ben Curdle and you took my Molly to the fair last time.'

Ben laughed, and Paul noticed again how crinkly his eyes were. No wonder Molly had missed him. She had said only a little to Paul, about the young man, as they took their excursions, but it had been enough for the child to realize that she had taken an uncommon liking to this fleeting visitor.

'Are you going to see Molly?' inquired Paul. Ben bent down to pick a stalk of grass and his face was red when he straightened up.

'Ah, maybe!' he answered, with carefully assumed indifference. Such cavalier behaviour annoyed young Paul.

'Well, you *did ought*!' he maintained stoutly. 'You never wrote, and you never wrote, and Molly looked out for a letter for *weeks and weeks*. She thought you were real mean, not writing.'

Ben's eyes widened at this vehement attack, but he answered equably enough.

'I'll look her up, Paul. Don't you fret.' He dusted down his black corduroys, and gave a sudden swift grin at the boy.

'Comin' to the fair tonight?' he asked.

'Yes, rather!' said the boy warmly.

'See you then,' nodded Ben. He sketched a salute and set off, with long rapid strides towards the lane which led to Lulling Woods, leaving Paul standing gazing after him.

The child watched until the energetic black legs, the

dazzling white shirt, and the bright neckerchief vanished between The Two Pheasants and the Piggotts' cottage.

He's got his best clothes on, thought young Paul sagaciously. And he's going the right way!

And, savouring these very satisfactory portents, he returned slowly to his gate.

Ben's heart was light as he swung along through the meadows that lay before the heights of Lulling Woods. In the sunshine the buttercups were opening fast, interlacing their gold with the earlier silver of the daisies. For the sheer joy of it young Ben left the white path and trod a parallel one through the gilded grass, watching his black shoes turn yellow with the fallen pollen.

The field fell gently downhill to his left, tipping its little, secret, underground streams towards the River Pleshy, a mile distant. Dotty Harmer's cottage was the only house to be seen here, basking among the buttercups like a warmly golden cat.

Dotty herself was in the garden, a straw hat of gigantic proportions crowning her untidy thatch of hair. She waved to the young man and called out something which he could not catch.

He waved back civilly.

'Nice day, ma'am,' he shouted, for good measure.

'Rum ol' trout,' he added to himself, noting her eccentric appearance. 'Not quite the ticket I should think. Or else gentry.'

He forgot her as soon as the cottage was behind him. A bend in the path brought him to a stile at the entrance to Lulling Woods. It was nearly a mile of steep climbing, he knew, before he would emerge on to the open heathland where The Drovers' Arms stood.

His spirits were buoyant. So she'd missed him! She hadn't

forgotten him! Everything pointed to happiness. He forged up the narrow path, slippery with a myriad pine needles, as though his feet were winged.

It was very cool and quiet in the woods after the bland sunshine of the meadows. Above him the topmost twigs of the trees whispered interminably. An occasional shaft of sunlight penetrated the foliage and lit up the bronze trunks of the pines, touching them with fire. A grey squirrel, spry after its winter sleep, startled Ben by scampering across his path. It darted up a tree with breathtaking ease, and the young man watched it leaping from bough to bough, as light and airy as a puff of grey smoke.

The primroses were out, starring the carpet of tawny dead leaves, and the bluebells, soon to spread their misty veil, now crouched in bud among their glossy leaves in tight pale knots. The faint, but heady, perfume of a spring woodland was to stay with Ben for the rest of his life, and was connected, for ever, with a lover's happiness.

At last, exhausted by his own fervent speed, Ben was obliged to rest, and it was then that his feverishly high spirits suffered their first check. What had that boy said? Molly thought him 'real mean' not to write? His heart sank like a plummet, and he kicked moodily at the log upon which he had sunk.

Suppose she was fed up with him? Suppose she refused to see him because he hadn't bothered to get in touch with her? She was a real pretty girl, and in a pub she'd have plenty of followers. Back flocked his familiar fears to torment him with renewed savagery.

And if she did speak to him again, what of it? What could he offer her? It was a poor sort of life he led in the caravan. A decent girl, used to service in a great house like the Bassets', and living in a snug little cottage on Thrush Green, wouldn't be likely to take up with a travelling-fair man. Might just as well mate up with some good-for-nothing tinker or scissor-grinder, thought Ben gloomily, now as dejected as he was formerly elated.

Be different, he told himself, rubbing salt into his wounds, if there was any chance of Gran taking him into partnership, as she had once suggested. But what hope of that now? Hardly spoke to a chap, he thought morosely, remembering their almost silent dinner together an hour or two before.

Suddenly overcome with despair he let his unhappy head fall into his hands. His fingers knotted and writhed in and out of his wiry black hair and he groaned aloud. An inquisitive robin settled on a twig nearby and surveyed his agony with an unfeeling bright eye.

What should he do? What should he do? he begged himself as he rocked his hot head this way and that. Go on and be humiliated, or turn tail and slink back to Thrush Green like the coward he was? He looked up and caught sight of his companion whose beady eye was still cocked upon this strange creature's sufferings.

It was at this moment that two thoughts combined to make poor Ben's way clear.

'She missed you!' came one comforting whisper. And hard upon its heels came a great cry from Ben himself, as he jumped to his feet.

'I've got to see her! Just to see her! Whatever comes of it, I'll see her first!'

He took to the uphill path again, but now his feet were leaden. Only his fierce single-minded passion to see the girl once more helped him to ignore the swarm of doubts which stung and plagued his progress.

He drew towards the edge of Lulling Woods and emerged from their dusk into the clear sunshine of the open heath. Bees hummed among the gorse flowers and two larks vied with each other as they sang a duet high in the blue air.

Not fifty yards away, where four modest tracks met, The Drovers' Arms stood waiting for him behind its neat strip of mown grass. The door was shut, no smoke rose from the chimneys, and not a soul was in sight. Only two grey and white geese rose menacingly from the shade of a low hedge, and advanced, with necks stretched out ominously, towards the unhappy young man.

But the windows were open, he noticed, and, very faintly, he could hear the sound of dishes being clattered in the kitchen at the rear of the house. A young clear voice began to sing, and Ben's heart turned over.

He took a great shuddering breath, raised his head, and set off to meet his fate.

8. A Chapter of Accidents

'Not bad! Not bad at all,' pronounced Ella Bembridge, dabbing parsley sauce from her chin with a hand-woven napkin.

Pink with praise, Dimity Dean carried the empty dish into the kitchen, returning with bananas in custard. The two friends hitched their wheel-back chairs to the table again and continued their meal and their gossiping.

'I must say,' said Ella, between succulent mouthfuls, 'that Winnie Bailey wears well. What must she be? Nearly seventy?' There was a slightly grudging note in her voice which did not escape her sensitive friend's notice.

'Oh, hardly that, dear,' she answered, in mollifying tones. 'And of course she's had a very *sheltered* life, being married, you know.'

Ella nodded, somewhat comforted.

'Time he gave up, if you ask me. That young fellow could

do worse than settle here, and he seemed fairly competent,
I thought. Inclined to take himself a bit seriously,' added
Ella, remembering her hasty dismissal from the morning
surgery. 'Likes to think he's the only one with any work to
do – but there you are! That's the way with everyone
today.'

'It might be rather dull for a young man at Thrush
Green –' began Dimity, but was cut short.

'*Dull?*' boomed her friend. 'What's *dull* about Thrush
Green? And anyway, if I'm not a Dutchman, he'll be marrying before long. He's been making sheep's eyes at Ruth
Bassett ever since the cocktail party Joan and Edward gave
this spring.'

'Now, Ella darling,' protested Dimity, with ineffectual
severity, 'that's really too naughty of you! I'm sure you're
imagining things. Ruth has been much too upset to look at
anyone else.'

'Doesn't stop him looking at her, does it?' persisted Ella
stoutly. She pushed aside her plate, took out the battered
tobacco tin, and rolled one of her monstrous cigarettes.
Dimity considered this possible romance as her friend blew
smoke upon the remains of the food. It might well be true.
Darling Ella' was wonderfully astute in matters like this. It
would be the best possible thing for poor little Ruth, thought
Dimity, her eyes filling as her sympathetic heart was pleasurably wrung. For once Ella noticed her friend's over-bright
eyes, and remembering Doctor Lovell's remark about heavy
lifting, she spoke with bluff kindness.

'Here, young Dim, you get along to bed and have your
rest. I'll wash up today. You look a bit done-up.'

Such unaccustomed consideration caused the tears to
hover perilously at the brink of Dimity's blue eyes.

'Are you sure, darling? You're so good to me.'

'Rubbish!' roared Ella cheerfully, crashing plates together

like tinkling cymbals. The custard spoon fell with a glutinous thwack upon the rush mat at their feet and the water jug slopped generously upon the polished table, as Ella bent her back, grunting heavily, to retrieve the spoon.

'Soon have everything ship-shape and Bristol fashion,' she said heartily, emerging red-faced from her exertions. 'Up you go for an hour.'

'But what about that stuff you wanted to dye? Can you manage it alone?' quavered Dimity, hovering about the table.

'Easily!' replied Ella, screwing the linen table mats into tight balls before thrusting them into the table drawer. Dimity averted her gaze. Dear Ella, so good-hearted, but so clumsy! Depend upon it there would be as much work to do clearing up after Ella's ministrations as if she had done the job herself, thought Dimity. But she mustn't be disloyal, she told herself, and really it was uncommonly thoughtful of Ella to offer to do these chores she so hated.

'Very well, dear,' she said gratefully. 'I'll go up, if you insist! But do put on your rubber gloves!'

She mounted the creaking stairs to the little bedroom above and turned a stoical ear to a dreadful crash, followed by a muttered imprecation, which shook the cottage.

'As long as it isn't mother's fruit bowl,' thought Dimity anxiously, and climbed resignedly under the eiderdown.

Having washed up the glass, silver, and china, and carefully stacked the sticky casserole, caked with parsley sauce, a saucepan equally encrusted with mashed potato, a parsley cutter, a stained board on which the herb had been cut, and various other utensils used in the preparation of the meal, all upon the draining-board to await Dimity's ministrations later, Ella felt aglow with righteousness.

It was really rather pleasant to have the kitchen to herself, she decided. She filled an enormous two-handled saucepan with water and set it on the gas-stove ready for the dyeing. The rubber gloves annoyed her. They were slippery, and her hands felt clumsy in them, but she realized that she had better obey Doctor Lovell's injunctions if she were going to handle her painting materials.

She set about mixing the dye in an old enamel bowl. It was a beautiful deep red, and by the time it had been added to the hot water, it looked as luscious as wine.

Ella tested a scrap of the natural-coloured linen she proposed to steep in it. It came out a satisfyingly rich shade and Ella sighed with pleasure. Little by little she let the length of stuff slide into the bubbling brew until it was all submerged.

As she stood by it in the quiet kitchen waiting for the allotted time to pass she became conscious of the sounds of the fair. She could hear the occasional shout of one man to another as they rigged up the booths or steadied machinery. There was a steady chugging noise which she guessed was the engine which provided the power for the roundabout and switchback. Everything was tested carefully before the evening, and Ella could well imagine Mrs Curdle making her rounds, ebony stick in hand, as she had done for so many May-days before the fair opened to the customers on Thrush Green. It would be a pity if the rumour proved true, thought Ella, stirring her cauldron like some stout, preoccupied witch.

Time was up. Ella turned the gas off, cursing the rubber gloves which added to her habitual clumsiness. She surveyed the great pot with a doubtful eye. It was very heavy, she knew from long experience, and usually Dimity helped her lift it into the sink.

It was on the tip of her tongue to hail her unsuspecting friend above her with her usual hearty exuberance. Dimity, she knew, would come readily tripping down the stairs, only too anxious to be of use. But today, with the milk of human kindness still pulsing its somewhat bewildered way through her veins, Ella decided, generously, to manage on her own.

Giving a tug to her maddening rubber gloves Ella approached the stove. She gripped the two handles and gave a mighty heave. It certainly was heavy and she wondered, for a split second, if she should replace it.

But pride overcame caution. She gave a determined stagger towards the sink before disaster overtook her.

Whether, as she afterwards maintained, the confounded rubber gloves slipped along the handles and shot the contents downward, or whether she caught her foot in the coconut matting, or whether, in fact, both calamities occured, she was never quite clear. But, in one agonizing moment, the pot overturned, and fell upside-down to the floor, cascading boiling dye down poor Ella's legs and draping her ankles and feet in searingly hot wet linen, which acted like some ghastly cleaving blood-red poultice.

Her screams brought Dimity pell-mell downstairs to stand aghast at the scene. Ella was disengaging herself from her fiendish encumbrances, her face contorted with pain.

'Oh, Ella, Ella!' was all poor Dimity could say, putting her thin arms around her suffering friend's shoulders. It was Ella herself who directed operations.

'Give me a hand getting my skirt and stockings off,' she ordered, gasping painfully. She stumbled to the kitchen chair, once white but now mottled with claret-coloured splashes, and began to fumble at her shoes. They were filled with the hot liquid and the metal eyelet holes were searing her flesh. Dimity collected her wits and helped her to strip off her garments, but as soon as she saw the scalded flesh, already beginning to blister, her face crumpled.

'Oh, poor Ella, poor darling Ella! I'll run and get Doctor Lovell. You simply must have a doctor!'

'He's out,' panted Ella, still struggling with a mammoth suspender, 'and anyway, we're going to wash this dye off before anyone starts messing about with my legs. Get some stuff out of the medicine chest, for pity's sake!'

Dimity fled to the bathroom and returned with the tiny first-aid box.

'There's this lotion that Dotty Harmer made up for your hands. D'you think that would help?' she asked, holding up an evil-looking green liquid in a shaking hand.

'Talk sense!' snapped Ella, with pardonable irritation. 'D'you want gangrene to set in?'

Dimity rummaged frantically again, tears falling from her eyes.

'Which it may well do, anyway,' went on Ella morosely, surveying a crimson ankle. 'And I'll be stumping about Thrush Green on my knees for the rest of my life,' she continued, warming up to her theme, and becoming garrulous, now that the first shock was over and she had a sympathetic audience.

Dimity could bear no more.

'I'm going now,' she exclaimed. 'You can't possibly see to that alone. I'll help you to the bathroom and you can swab it with cotton wool if you like, but you must have proper medical attention. Shall I ring the hospital for an ambulance?'

'Good God, Dim!' shouted Ella, shocked at this ruthless suggestion. 'Do you want to kill me?'

For Ella's conception of hospitals was two-fold. In the first place, she looked upon them as large, disinfectant-reeking establishments, provided by society, for the hygienic segregation of those about to quit this world; and secondly, as convenient and practical schools for medical men who literally had their raw material at their finger-ends. The thought of entering one alarmed her far more than the actual accident.

Together the two women struggled to the bathroom, which was situated, luckily, on the ground floor. Dimity fetched Ella's dressing-gown, established her on a stool by the bath, and left her friend to bathe her legs and feet in tepid water. She was not at all happy about this, but Ella, now secretly near to tears with pain, shock, and the truly awful suggestion of hospital treatment, was becoming voluble and obstreperous.

'I'm sure we should be putting oil, or a paste of bicarbonate of soda, or something like that on it,' protested poor Dimity, one distracted hand ruffling her hair. 'If only I could remember what I learnt during the war! I used to know it all so well – and now I can only remember how to deal with incendiary bombs! Poor Ella!'

'If you're going for the doctor, then go!' burst out her much-tried companion. And, without another word, Dimity fled for help.

Doctor Bailey was dozing in the sunny garden when Dimity pealed agitatedly at the bell.

Dimly, through the comfortable wrappings of slumber which surrounded him, the doctor became conscious of women's voices in the hall. Someone was pouring forth a torrent of words while his wife was doing her best to soothe the visitor. Rousing himself from his chair Doctor Bailey went in from the sunshine to investigate the commotion.

'It's Ella!' burst forth Dimity, as soon as he came in view.

'She has had an accident,' put in his wife swiftly. 'I'm going along to see if I can help. There's no need for you to be disturbed.'

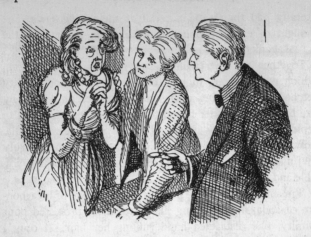

'She's most dreadfully scalded —' began Dimity, in a tear-ful gabble.

'Scalded, eh?' interjected the doctor. 'I'll come along.' He reached for the black bag which always stood in readiness on the hall table. His wife made another attempt to return him to his disturbed rest.

'Let me go first, and if we need you I promise I'll come back,' she said, laying a hand on her husband's arm. He disengaged it gently.

'It's no distance, my dear, and we mustn't neglect an old friend like Ella when she's in trouble.' He lifted the bag and made for the front door, followed by Dimity twittering her thanks and fears. Mrs Bailey, knowing when she was beaten, wisely said no more, but watched them make their way to the gate through the warm flower-scented garden.

Ella was still sitting in the bathroom when the doctor arrived. He took one look at his patient whose teeth were now chattering with cold and shock, and said firmly:

'Bed for you, my dear. Come along.'

'What, on a lovely afternoon like this?' protested Ella.

'Yes, indeed. Dimity, put the kettle on and make a cup of tea for both of you.' He turned to Ella. 'I'll help you upstairs and Dimity can give you a hand later on. Those legs want dressing straight away.'

Slowly they mounted the stairs. Ella's massive arm was thrown round the doctor's shoulders and it was as much as he could do to support her weight up the crooked staircase, across the landing, and into her bedroom.

Dimity, having put the kettle on, returned to help her friend undress and put on her nightgown while the doctor unpacked his bag.

'And she'll want that dressing-gown too,' ordered the doctor. 'Keep her warm, my dear.'

An ear-splitting whistle from below warned the company that the kettle was boiling and Dimity moved away leaving Ella to the ministrations of their old friend.

The kitchen was in an unbelievable condition of chaos, as poor Dimity saw as she set out teacups upon a tray. She lifted the soaking linen into the sink and put the great saucepan outside the back door. The mat was ruined and the walls, chairs, and scrubbed table-top spattered with crimson dye. There was an hour's hard work waiting for her here, decided Dimity sadly.

As she lifted the tray her eye fell upon the mound of revoltingly sticky utensils which Ella had left at lunchtime. She sighed bravely and made her way to the door. It was perhaps a good thing that domestic martyrdom was a commonplace in Dimity Dean's life.

'She'll do,' said Doctor Bailey ten minutes later. 'Not as bad as I first thought – but you're to stay there until Lovell's had a look at you. A shock like that takes more out of you than you realize.'

He turned a shrewd and kindly eye upon Dimity.

'And you'd better have an early night too,' he said. 'Get as much sleep as you can. Both of you.'

'On May the first?' cried Dimity. 'You know the fair keeps us all awake for hours! Really, I do think it's too bad to allow that dreadful noise to go on as it does!'

'Only once a year, Dim,' pointed out Ella from the bed. 'And probably the last time anyway.'

'I hope not,' said Doctor Bailey, gathering his things together. 'Stuff your ears with cotton wool, if you must! But don't forget – early bed!'

He parted from Dimity at the front door.

'There's nothing to worry about,' he assured her, noticing her anxious face. 'Ella's got the constitution of a horse.'

He waved farewell, and, somewhat comforted, Dimity Dean returned to the upheaval in the kitchen.

The dazzle of Thrush Green after the shade of Ella's bedroom was almost too much for the doctor. His head bumped strangely and the trees and caravans and busy fair-folk blurred together in a giddy whirling motion.

He stopped by a fence and steadied himself against it. His bag seemed uncommonly heavy and he set it down carefully, closing his eyes in case vertigo overcame him.

'Damn, damn, damn!' swore the doctor furiously to himself. 'Twenty yards' walk, one simple case, and I'm useless!'

He leant dizzily against the fence, praying that his wife should not happen to look out from their gate and see his helplessness. Another minute and he would be perfectly all right, he told himself.

A voice spoke, so close to him that he was startled.

'You all right, doctor?' It was Mr Piggott, lately come from The Two Pheasants which had shut its doors some half-hour or so before. A smell of beer and plug tobacco emanated from him, so strongly that the doctor was partially revived by it.

'Yes, yes. I'm all right, many thanks, Piggott. Found the sunshine a bit dazzling, that's all.'

He was surprised, and touched too, to see the expression of concern on the old rapscallion's normally surly countenance, and even more surprised when he lifted up his black bag for him and accompanied him to his gate.

'Well, that's very kind of you, to be sure,' he said, when they arrived. For want of anything better to say he waved towards the fair.

'Are you going tonight?'

'Me? Not likely,' growled Piggott, with his usual venom. 'I'll be glad to see the back o' this lot, I can tell 'ee. Nothing but a set of rogues and thieves. Be a good riddance when they clears out tomorrow.' He hitched his trousers up viciously and ambled away through the offending collection of caravans to his work, leaving the doctor pondering on this exhibition of both sides of his neighbour's nature.

'How was she?' first asked his wife. And then, in the same breath: 'You shouldn't have gone. You're over-tired.'

The doctor roused himself to speak calmly.

'Ella's not too bad. I've left her in bed and the burns will keep till Lovell can see her in the morning.'

He had put down the black bag, as he had done so many times, upon the hall table; but this time his hand remained resting upon it as he faced his wife.

'Come and sit down,' urged Mrs Bailey. 'You really shouldn't have gone.'

'I'm glad I went,' replied the doctor steadily, patting the bag as one might a much-loved dog. 'It's helped me to come to a decision.'

'About Doctor Lovell?'

'About Doctor Lovell,' agreed the doctor. 'I shall offer him a partnership tonight.'

9. At The Drovers' Arms

MOLLY PIGGOTT sang as she washed up the glasses in the back kitchen of The Drovers' Arms.

She was alone in the house, for as soon as the bar had shut at two o'clock, Ted Allen, the landlord, and his wife Bessie, had driven off to Lulling, in their twenty-year-old Baby Austin, to do the week-end shopping.

'We'll be back in an hour or so, love,' fat, rosy Bessie had called from the car, 'in time to let you get away real early, as it's fair day. Keep your eyes open for the laundry van. He's supposed to be calling about three – but you know what he is!'

They had rattled off leaving Molly to enjoy the peaceful kitchen on her own. She was glad of her own company for she was in a state of great excitement.

Molly had been born at the little cottage on Thrush Green and, for her, May the first had always been the high-light of the year. The travelling fair had become associated for Molly with the most bewitching time of the country year, when hope, warmth, and colour flooded fields and gardens, and the hearts of men could not fail to be quickened by the glory around them. And this year the fair-day held a particular significance for Molly Piggott.

The memory of that lovely evening with Ben had warmed Molly throughout the year. She had been more attracted by the young man than she had realized, and she was aston-

ished at her own disappointment when she had failed to
hear from him.

She had continued to go about her daily affairs looking as
cheerful and as bustling as ever, but at heart she was sadly
perplexed. She cooked and cleaned, washed and mended,
weeded the garden and fed the hens, enduring the surly
company of her father with less equanimity than usual, and
escaping as often as she could to the haven of the Bassetts'
house across the green. Paul was an enormous comfort to
her, and although she was careful not to let too much slip
out about the dark young man who had taken her to the
fair, Paul's pertinent questions and shrewd guesswork soon
uncovered her secret.

He was genuinely sympathetic to poor Molly and hated
to know that she was in any way upset. Touched to the
heart by his warm-hearted solicitude Molly still tried to
treat the whole affair light-heartedly, but Paul was not to be
so easily put off.

'You should write to him,' said Paul decidedly, as they
walked together one afternoon to Dotty Harmer's to get the
eggs. The rain was slanting across the field, shrouding Lulling Woods in a grey veil. Paul strode through the puddles
in his gumboots. His sou'wester dripped upon his shiny
oilskins in little rivulets. One hand was thrust in his pocket
and the other comforted Molly's with a warm wet grasp.

'He may be a real nice man,' he continued judicially,
ignoring the torrents about him, 'but he can't know you're
worrying about him, or he'd come and see you.'

'I'm not worrying,' Molly had said, with a very good
imitation of a light laugh. 'And I can't write to him if I
don't know where the fair is, can I? Even if I wanted to –
which I don't!' she had added hastily.

'He should come,' maintained Paul stoutly. 'He must be a
friend because he gave you that brooch and he took you to

the fair. He should come and see you. Or he should send you a picture postcard of wherever the fair is.'

'Perhaps he's ill,' suggested Molly, making excuses for Ben against her will. 'Or maybe old Mrs Curdle don't like him wasting his time writing to girls. She's a proper ol' pip, they say, at keeping 'em all working.'

Paul, with a child's black and white conception of right and wrong, and having no interest in or recognition of those forgiving shades of grey with which adults confuse the issue, would have no excuses made for poor absent Ben.

He asked Molly whenever they met if she had heard from Ben, so that Molly grew more and more alarmed at the interest taken in her affairs, and dreaded lest the child should let fall some chance remark at home or anywhere else on Thrush Green. She knew, only too well, how quickly rumours spread in a small community and was horrified to think how a spark, so innocently dropped by sympathetic young Paul, would blaze a trail from Thrush Green to Lulling, to Nod and Nidden and all the little hamlets that clustered near the River Pleshy. As for her father, if he should come to hear of the evening out, let alone anything further, he was quite capable of making her life a misery with braggart threats and mean-spirited mockings.

'Don't you say a word now,' she had said severely to Paul one day when he had questioned her once more about the errant Ben. 'It's a secret, see? I wish I'd never said a word about him to you. I don't care all that about him anyway,' protested poor Molly, tossing her head.

'Then why do you wear that cornflower brooch every day?' Paul had answered mildly. For two pins Molly could have slapped the child, torn as she was between exasperation and affection. She did her best to speak calmly.

'Well, he was kind to me, Paul, and I likes to wear it to remind me of a lovely time. But there's no call for you to think I'm fretting, you know. And don't forget – what I've told you is a secret. Promise?'

'Promise,' echoed Paul solemnly, and he had kept his word.

But Molly had grown increasingly perturbed as the year slid from summer into winter. Her father's boorishness, his bouts of morose drinking, and her own disappointment over Ben's silence combined to make her life depressing. She almost dreaded going to the Bassetts' house in the winter months for then she and Paul were together indoors, often in the company of Joan and Edward, and Molly trembled lest Paul should forget his promise and reveal her feelings unintentionally. It was during the autumn that she heard about the post at The Drovers' Arms.

'They wants a girl as'll help in the bar and give them a hand in the house,' the milkman had told her one day. He was a cheerful fellow who always stopped for a word, and was fond of any lively buxom girl like Molly. He was a great favourite with most of the ladies on Thrush Green, though Dimity Dean had found him 'detestably familiar' once when she had been obliged to answer the door in her dressing-gown.

'Why tell me?' Molly had asked, with genuine interest.

'You're too good to waste away under this roof,' the man had said shrewdly. 'You'd see a bit of life up there. The Allens is real nice and homely. Food's good, pay's good, and home here for the week-end if you still wants to see old Happy Face!' He had jerked a thumb in the direction of Mr Piggott who was stirring up a bonfire in the church-yard.

'They won't want me,' said Molly. 'I've never done bar work.'

'You go and see 'em,' urged the milkman, patting her arm. 'I told 'em you'd be just the right sort of gal if they could persuade you. You think it over. Tell 'em I sent you up.'

She had turned this amazing offer over in her mind as she had gone about her duties that day, and had almost decided not to go. But that evening her father had been unbearable. He had pushed the piece of steak that the girl had cooked for him this way and that across his plate, prodding it with a fork and grumbling about its toughness, its meagre dimensions, and his daughter's poor cooking. That decided the matter for Molly. She had stood enough.

She said nothing at the time, but the next day she walked through the autumn woods to The Drovers' Arms and faltered out her willingness to take the post.

Ted and Bessie Allen were a boisterous, kindly pair, who took at once to the pretty girl whose character had been given them by the milkman. It was all quickly arranged. Molly was to live there from Monday night until Friday afternoon each week, and the week-ends were her own as Mrs Allen's brother came down from town each week-end and liked to help in the bar to earn his keep.

Mr Piggott was too flabbergasted at this *fait accompli* to make much comment. Joan Bassett was glad for the girl's sake for she knew that her home conditions were wretched, but glad too to know that Molly would come to help her at week-ends if ever she were needed.

And so the winter and spring had slipped by and Molly's spirits had risen as the good company and good living at the little pub had had their effect. She was willing, lively, and glowed with good health and fun, and became a great favourite with the customers.

No one would have thought that Molly Piggott had a care in the world. Her eyes sparkled, her curly hair sprang crisply above her clear white brow, and she tripped lightly about her business.

But the cornflower brooch was always pinned on her dress, and at night when she put it carefully away in the shell-encrusted box which had accompanied her to The Drovers' Arms her eyes would cloud as she remembered the young man who had asked her to be true but, alas, had forgotten to be true himself.

As May had approached she had become more and more excited. At least she would see him again. Not that she was going to run after him, she told herself! If he liked to come and find her – well, that was different.

And if he didn't come? Then she had her plans ready. There were several young men who called at the pub who had already suggested that she might honour them with her company at Thrush Green fair. To all she had given an evasive answer, praying secretly that Ben would have called for her long before the fair opened. But if he didn't come – and at this dreadful thought her spirits fell like a plummet – then she would go with the first young man who asked her, and she would see Ben again, and speak to him too. And woe betide that dark young breaker-of-hearts if he failed to clear up the mystery of a silence which had lasted a year!

All through the sparkling morning Molly had hoped and wondered, plotted and surmised. Ben would not be able to see her much before tea-time, she reckoned, for she knew that it took most of the day to prepare the fair and Mrs Curdle would see that there were no defaulters.

She had looked out the yellow spotted frock which she had worn the year before, and had polished her new black shoes with the high heels. She had tried a yellow ribbon across her dark hair and had approved of her reflection in the dim mirror in the little attic bedroom under the thatch. The ribbon lay now, beside the spotted frock, across the white counterpane.

Molly sang at the thought of the pretty things awaiting her upstairs. She would wash up, and then she would take up a jug of warm rainwater to her bedroom and wash herself in the blue-and-white bowl on the corner washstand. She would brush her hair till it frothed round her head and then tie the yellow ribbon smoothly across. And then, she told herself with a beating heart, dressed and freshly clean, she would sit in the sunshine and wait.

She glanced through the window at the trim garden. Heat waves shimmered across the pink-and-white apple blossom, and a few fragile petals fluttered down, in the heat, upon the forget-me-nots that clustered below. It was all so beautiful that Molly's song ceased abruptly as she stared.

She rested her plump arms along the edge of the sink. Soap-suds popped softly on the creamy skin. Her red frock, so soon to be changed for the immaculate yellow one above, was wet with her energetic splashings, and her curls clung damply against her brow.

'He'd have to come, a day like this,' whispered Molly to herself, gazing bemused at the view before her.

And, at that moment, Ben knocked upon the back door.

Outside, in the scorching sunshine, Ben waited anxiously. The heat beat back from the worn paint of the door. A blister or two had risen here and there, and in the vivid light Ben noticed minute iridescent specks freckling the paintwork, reminding him of the sheen on a pheasant's throat.

He was never to forget that endless moment of waiting, in the full murmurous beauty of May Day, the acrid smell of the hot paint-work mingling with the fragrance of the spring garden.

He heard the singing stop. There was a sudden silence,

and then the sound of footsteps on the stone-flagged floor. The door opened, and Ben's heart turned over.

There she stood, prettier than ever, her eyes sparkling with such radiance that Ben knew instantly that he need never have doubted his welcome.

'Ben!' breathed Molly rapturously, all preconceived ideas of a frigid approach to the errant young man melting at once as their eyes met.

Ben was unable to speak, but stood gazing at the corn-flower brooch at her neck.

'Ben!' repeated Molly, holding out two soapy hands and a striped tea towel. 'Come in out of the heat!'

Obediently, Ben stepped over the threshold into the cool shade of the kitchen. He was still speechless with joy and wild relief. But if his tongue was useless his arms were not. And throwing them round the tea towel, the wet frock, and his plump, lovely Molly, he hugged her until she gasped for breath.

After the first joy of meeting, Ben took another tea towel and helped the girl to wipe the glasses.

'And then we're going out,' he said firmly.

'But I can't, Ben, honest, I can't!' pleaded Molly. 'There's no one here to see the laundry man and there's the chicken-food to cook up, and the —'

Ben cut her short.

'Stick a note on the door for the laundry, and put the chickens' grub over the side of the hob. That won't hurt. We'll go up the common for a bit.'

'I've got to be here about five, though, just to see the others in. Then I'm free.'

'You must come and see my old Gran before the fair starts,' persisted Ben. 'I wants her to see you. You'll like her all right.' He gazed admiringly at Molly, whose brow was

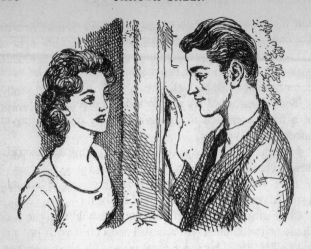

furrowed with trying to work out an afternoon's pro-
gramme which gave her as much time as possible with Ben
and yet saw her duties done.

'And what's more,' went on Ben, 'she'll like you!'

It all sounded alarmingly fast for Molly trying to keep
her head amidst this sudden whirl of events.

'I'll go and change my frock first,' she said, hoping to
escape to the peace of her bedroom for a few minutes in
order to collect her scattered wits. But Ben would have
none of it. They'd been apart for a year and now he had
found her again he had no intention of letting her out of his
sight.

'Come out now,' he urged. 'You look fine in that red
frock.'

'But it's all wet –' faltered Molly, displaying the splashes.

'Sun'll dry it,' said Ben firmly, spreading the tea towel
over a chair back. He turned, and, arms akimbo, surveyed
the girl as she stood thoughtfully by the sink, looking down
at her damp dress.

'Change your frock when you come back to the fair with me,' suggested Ben. Molly looked up, and catching sight of his crinkly dark eyes smiling at her, regained her usual sparkle.

'I didn't say I was coming to the fair, did I?' said Molly, turning wide eyes upon him. 'Not with you anyways. There's plenty of other young men have asked me lately, and I haven't said "Yes" or "No" to any of 'em.'

Ben was not to be foiled by these womanly wiles. After the months of doubting fears, culminating in the anguish of mind as he had walked through Lulling Woods in the heat of the day, it was as though he were now inoculated against all further torments. He knew, with a deep sense of wonder and inner comfort that was to remain with him all his life, that the girl before him was his for ever, to be as essential to him, and as much part of him, as his hand or eye.

It was this knowledge that gave him a new-found strength and gentleness. Nothing now could go wrong, he told himself, anywhere – ever – in the whole world!

He took the girl's hand and led her, laughing, to the door.

'Other men!' he scoffed exultantly. 'To hell with them! You're coming with me!'

And together they made their way out into the sunshine.

The common, which surrounded The Drovers' Arms, rose at one point to a cluster of beech trees which served as a landmark for miles around.

It was towards the trees that the two climbed through the dry fine grass, and when they reached the first welcome shade thrown by the outspread branches they sat down to talk.

From the little hill they had a clear view of the four roads that met at The Drovers' Arms, for Molly, despite her excitement, was still conscious of her mistress's injunction about the laundry and about 'keeping an eye' on the place. By settling here she salved her conscience enough to be able to give young Ben the major part of her attention.

The heat waves quivered across the view spread before them. A myriad winged insects hummed in the warm air, and far away, so high above that it was lost in blue air, a distant aeroplane droned drowsily.

Ben rested his arms on his knees, a grass between his teeth, and observed the mighty hulk of a steam-roller, drawn up in a clearing at the side of the road directly below them. A froth of Queen Anne's lace had grown up round the rusty wheels, and the sun glinted on the brass horse which ornamented the front. Soon its winter rest would come to an end, for with the May sunshine would come the time for tarring, and the sleeping monster would be tugged from the clinging greenery which softened its primitive and grotesque lines and be roused into life by fire kindled in its belly. With the rumbling of the giant about the quaking lanes the people of Lulling would know that high summer had really come.

Tired with their climb, and with all that had happened to them, Ben and Molly spoke little at first, content to be in each other's company and enjoy the quiet loveliness that echoed their own bliss. But gradually their tongues loosened and they began to exchange news of the long year behind them.

Ben listened with pity and anger to Molly's account of life at the cottage on Thrush Green, and admired secretly the sturdy common sense with which she had faced her difficulties, devoid of any self-pity for her conditions. But his heart smote him even more poignantly when she put a hand upon his sunburnt arms and said:

'And then you never came! And, worse still, you never wrote! I did think you'd send a letter, p'raps.'

Ben took a deep breath. The shameful secret would have to be told, and better now than later on.

'I can't write, Moll, and that's the truth,' he said looking away from her. A yard away the blue broken shell of a bird's egg had become speared upon a tall grass, and swayed gently, like some exotic harebell.

'Can't write?' echoed Molly in amazement. He turned to her swiftly, and Molly's heart was shaken at the pain in his face.

'Well, I never had much schooling. Being with the fair, see. We was always on the move. I can read a bit, but all the schools I went to seemed to do different writing and some-how I never sort of mastered it.'

His fingers plucked nervously at the grass and Molly covered them with her own.

'You don't want to worry about a little thing like that,' she said stoutly. 'I knows dozens as can't write. And anyway I can easy teach you. 'Twouldn't take you more than a week or two to get the hang of it.'

'I'd like that,' nodded young Ben earnestly. 'And Gran'd be pleased.'

He went on to tell her about the old lady and the hopes he had of being taken into partnership. He told her about the work of the fair, the earnings he had, and the improvements he would make if he had any say in the future running of the business.

Molly listened intently. The life of the fair had always attracted her, and the account of the hard work which lay behind the glitter held no fears for her. If that were to be her life, she would relish it. She was used to tough conditions, she welcomed change and movement with the natural excitement of youth, and she knew too that wherever the young man before her chose to go she would want to go too. But she was, nevertheless, a little taken aback to hear him describe the alterations he would make to his caravan for their future comfort.

'But, Ben,' she protested, 'you're taking a lot for granted.'

He looked at her bewildered face and, for a moment, all his old doubts assailed him again.

'Maybe I'm asking too much,' he said soberly. 'Girls like you, with a steady job and a home and that, would find our everlasting traipsin' the roads a come-down. 'Tisn't fair perhaps to ask you to take on a rough chap from a fair, and never have no comfort.'

He was lying full length upon the grass, his chin propped on his fists, and now he looked up with such utter misery at Molly that she caught her breath.

'But, Moll,' he pleaded, 'what'll I do if you won't come?'

There was a little silence, stirred only by the summer murmuring about them, while poor Ben waited for his answer.

'I'll come,' promised Molly, at last.

10. Sam Curdle is Tempted

WHILE Ben Curdle lay, lapped in bliss, upon the grassy heath above Lulling Woods, his cousin Sam was facing a domestic squall at Thrush Green.

His wife Bella was in a fine fury. She confronted him now, her eyes flashing. Her massive bosom heaved under the tight red dress as she railed. As usual it was money that she demanded.

'I tell you, Bella,' protested Sam, 'I'm broke. I give you your whack last week. What you done with that lot?' His face was as red as his wife's.

'You had plenty yesterday morning,' screamed Bella.

'You hand some over. It's for your kids' clothes – that's all I'm asking for! D'you want to see 'em barefoot?'

Sam swore softly under his breath, but put a grimy hand in his pocket.

'That's the lot!' he growled, flinging two filthy pound notes on to the table. Bella swooped upon them and rammed them into her shiny black handbag.

'About time,' was her comment. 'We gets paid tonight anyway – no need for you to be mean all of a sudden.'

She put her head out of the doorway and yelled to her three children who were playing with a skewbald pony in the shade of the lime trees.

'Give over! We're going down Lulling. Come and get your faces wiped!'

She turned to have a parting shot at her husband. He was kicking moodily at the table leg and his face was black as thunder.

'If you're short of money, why don't you ask the old girl for more? You earns it, don't you? You're all the same, you Curdles! Afraid to say a word for yourselves against her. Under her thumb, the lot of you, under her thumb!'

And, still heaving with indignation, Bella descended the steps of the caravan to find her brood.

Sam lay back upon the garish cretonne cushions which Bella had made for the long wall-seat of the caravan, and cursed his luck. He cursed Bella and her tongue, the children and their everlasting wants, and his own feebleness in parting with the two pound notes.

These had been earmarked for the afternoon's betting, and now the outlook seemed hopeless. Sam gazed blackly at the ceiling above him where two flies waltzed erratically around Bella's pink-fringed lamp-shade. Give her her due, Sam admitted, as his temper cooled and the peace of the afternoon crept upon him, she kept the place nice, nag though she did.

His eyes wandered to the flowery curtains that matched the cushions below his head, to the pink rug that she had made, and the new plastic tablecloth with its scarlet-and-black design. When you thought that it had once been an old bus, Sam mused, it hadn't turned out a bad little home. Bit cramped, of course, now, with the three kids, but if the horses did their stuff maybe they'd be able to get a bigger caravan to live in – a real flash job, with plenty of chrome and a bay window with latticed panes.

The thought of the horses reminded Sam painfully of his predicament. He sat up and pulled the newspaper towards him morosely. Running a black-edged finger-nail down the racing column his gloom returned.

Yes, there they were, all right! Both the beauties that young chap had tipped him, Rougemont and Don John. One in the three-thirty and the other in the four-thirty, and here he was with ninepence halfpenny in his pocket! Sam swore anew.

The fair had stopped for two days, earlier in the week, at South Fenny, a village in Oxfordshire famous for its racing stables. In the pub Sam had been in conversation with one of the stable lads, an Irishman whose eloquence had impressed Sam deeply.

'Can't go wrong, my boy,' he had said earnestly to the traveller. 'They've both been readied for the Newbury meeting, and I know for a fact the stables are backing 'em. Remember the names now. Rougemont and Don John!'

'Don John!' Sam had said derisively, anxious to appear as knowledgeable as his adviser. 'Why, he ran like a cow at Lingfield!'

The Irishman brushed this aside with a testy wave of his hand.

'But I'm telling you, they were saving him for Newbury, getting him down in the handicap. Put all you can find on 'em, and you'll never regret it. Don't forget now – Rougemont and Don John. They're worth a fortune to you!'

Sam had bought him a drink for luck and had written the two names down on the edge of a newspaper. And now, here they were, both of them, running on the same afternoon and he had nothing to put on them.

He rose to his feet and went outside into the quivering sunshine. Across Thrush Green he could see the small stone house where Ernie Bender lived and worked, and where he laid bets for the lucky ones who had the money to take it to him.

Ernie Bender's house stood next door to that belonging to Ella Bembridge and Dimity Dean. It stood well back in a garden shady with plum and apple trees, and in the front window a notice said:

E. BENDER

BOOT AND SHOE REPAIRS

The inhabitants of Thrush Green were glad of Ernie Bender. He ministered to heels and soles, footballs, harness, handbags, and suitcases. In fact, as he was quick to tell his customers, he would 'have a go at anything made of leather – but it must be leather, mind! I won't waste my time on your plastic stuff!' Over the years he had stitched Doctor Bailey's black bag, Paul's pram hood, the netballs at the village school, saddles and bridles for Joan and Ruth when they were small, and kept in trim the footwear that passed and repassed his window as the various owners went about their business on Thrush Green.

He was a tiny gnome-like man who wore half-spectacles made of steel and peered over them at the view through his window as he sat on a high stool at his bench. Not much escaped those long-sighted eyes and he had been known to summon a running child to tell him that his sole was worn through and that his mother had better let him see to it right away.

His passion was horse-racing and he had an account with a bookmaker in Lulling. Many of his customers took their bets to Ernie Bender along with their boots, and found he was always ready to talk about racing memories or prospects for a coming race day, his eyes gleaming as brightly as the steel spectacles which rested on his diminutive nose.

Sam knew him well. It was there that Sam had proposed to go, sauntering casually behind the screen of caravans and booths to dodge Bella's and the old lady's eye, to put ten shillings each way on both Rougemont and Don John.

The bright sun mocked his despair and the peaceful scene before him only infuriated Sam still further. He cast round in his mind for any hope of a loan from one or other of the Curdle tribe, but it was hopeless, he knew.

In the first place this was Friday afternoon when purses and pockets were almost empty at Curdle's fairground. Tonight was pay-night, the brightest spot in the week. If only Rougemont and Don John had been entered on tomorrow's card, thought Sam!

As if to emphasize the callousness of time, St Andrew's clock let fall three silvery notes. Sam's fury flared anew. Another half-hour and Rougemont would be off!

'And he'll go like an arrow, my boy,' the Irishman had sworn solemnly. 'Nothing can stop him. He can't fail!'

The words echoed in Sam's ears infuriatingly. And he'd probably start at odds of eight to one, too, Sam told himself. And where was his money? Snug in Bella's bag. It was enough to make you take to wife-beating, that it was!

He looked up at the implacable face of St Andrew's clock and made a decision. He'd done it before and no one was any the wiser. He'd do it again. What if it did seem like stealing? If old Gran was too mean to pay him right, then she deserved to have a bit pinched now and again.

No, not pinched, he told himself hastily, as a vision of the tribe-leader's awe-inspiring face floated before him. Borrowing, let's say – just a little advance on what would be given him by right tonight. He could slip it back in the drawer sometime, just as easy as he could slip it out.

His stomach was queasy at the thought of his mission, for Sam was the most chicken-hearted of the Curdles. Only his passion for betting could render him brave enough to undertake the deed.

Old Ma, he knew, would be inspecting the fair, to see that all was in order before the evening opening. She did the routine job thoroughly, tugging at guy ropes, surveying the prizes, straightening notices, and going the rounds of each booth and stall minutely. The little menagerie was inspected with particular rigour, for Mrs Curdle was fond, as well as proud, of the pets exhibited and their food and comfort dare not be neglected.

Sam made his way as casually as he could across the grass. He did not walk directly towards Mrs Curdle's caravan, but wove his way, with seeming indifference, between the caravans clustered near the church.

Sitting on the steps of one of them he discovered Rosie, his young cousin. She was feeding her baby, patting its back gently and humming to herself as she rocked to and fro. She might have been the incarnation of spring itself, with her fair hair and pink-and-white skin, but Sam had no time to waste on aesthetic matters.

'Seen Ma?' he asked urgently.

The girl looked up at him dreamily.

'Saw her going in the animals,' she answered vaguely. 'Couldn't say when though. I been busy.'

She returned her gaze to the infant's face, smiling at it so blissfully that Sam knew he was forgotten at once.

The clock said ten past three. Sam slipped like a shadow among the booths, taking care to avoid his fellows, and came warily towards his goal.

Mrs Curdle had indeed started on her round of inspection that afternoon, but she had not completed it.

The burning pain, which now seemed to be her constant companion, had attacked her with spiteful severity soon after the silent meal with Ben.

After he had gone she had rested a little, and then had roused herself to wash up. She had been too engrossed with her own sufferings to give much heed to Ben, but as she flung the washing-up water into the sunlight she had caught sight of his slim figure striding across the shining grass, and all her old love for him had suddenly welled up.

He was George all over again, as straight, as handsome – the apple of her eye! Her pain forgotten, she watched him as he spoke to a little boy.

'Time he had one of his own!' she thought to herself and mused on the idea of her young George being a grand-father. She watched him turn towards the sun and set off purposefully towards the lane that led to Lulling Woods.

She could see now that he was dressed in his best, and she could see too, now that the sun shone full upon his face, that it was alight with excitement. Instantly, she knew the answer to those long silences and dark moods which had estranged them for the past months and marvelled that she had not guessed before.

'So it's a girl,' nodded old Mrs Curdle to herself, returning to the caravan. 'Just as simple as that – a girl!'

She had pondered upon this, sitting heavily on the side of

her bed and watching a finger of sunlight pick its way over the gleaming plates on the dresser.

She felt both sadness and delight at this revelation – sadness because she knew that Ben could never be wholly hers again, as he had been for almost the whole of his twenty years, and delight because it meant happiness for the boy.

Despite his youth she knew he would want to marry almost at once, as his father had done. She only prayed that he had chosen more wisely. If he had – if she were a girl with courage and gaiety, it would be the making of Ben.

'This'll change his ways,' the old lady told herself. 'Nothing like love for brightening up a young man. He'll work twice as hard with a wife to keep.'

She saw, shrewdly enough, that Ben's well-being would react on the fortunes of the fair and her heart was comforted by the thought that the business which she loved so well might yet flourish.

She heaved herself upright, took her ebony stick in hand, and set out upon her rounds.

Inside the menagerie tent Mrs Curdle found only one person attending to the animals' needs. Rachel was twelve years old, sister to Rosie the young mother who nursed her baby in the sunshine near at hand.

Their father was Mrs Curdle's nephew, a blond giant of a man, for whom she had little respect. It was he who should have been at hand, for he was in charge of the menagerie; but, more often than not these days, Rachel was left to attend to things.

She was a willing child and Mrs Curdle was fond of her. She spoke affectionately to her now, peering through the murk after the vivid light outside.

'And how's my Rachel?'

'Fine, Gran,' answered the child. She held up a jug and Mrs Curdle nodded approval. The girl was going methodically from cage to cage filling the water bowls. The faintly acrid smell of animals hung in the air.

'Where's your dad?' asked Mrs Curdle.

'Don't know.'

'He been in yet?'

'No. Over The Two Pheasants, I think.'

Mrs Curdle snorted and bent to inspect the toy house in which a frenzy of white mice lived and loved.

'Not enough sawdust,' was her comment.

'I can't find none, Gran,' confessed the child earnestly. 'I been looking all over. Dad said he'd get some this morning –'

'Your dad wants sorting out,' broke in the old lady. 'Leaving you to do his job!'

Her voice had a steely ring and the child trembled.

Mrs Curdle took a deep breath as though to continue her tirade, when suddenly she crumpled and fell forward. The ebony stick dropped from her hand, and, to the child's horror, the old lady slumped into a massive heap on the trampled grass.

The child fell on her knees beside her.

'Gran, Gran!' she whispered in terror, staring at the closed eyes.

Mrs Curdle's lips moved. From very far away, it seemed to the girl, her voice could be heard.

'I'm all right, my dear. Don't 'ee be frightened. I'll be better in a minute. Here, hold my hand.'

She gripped the child's hand in a grasp so fierce that the girl almost cried out.

'I'll get Dad! I'll get Rose! Gran, let me go, and I'll get someone!'

'You'll stop here,' said the small voice, but there was an implacable note in it that told the girl that she must stay.

A dreadful silence pervaded the stuffy tent. Only the small squeaks and twitters from the animals and the heavy laboured breathing of the prostrate woman could be heard. Gradually strength returned to Mrs Curdle. She opened her eyes and sat up, though her head dropped in an alarming manner.

'Get us up, girl,' whispered the old lady, releasing her at last.

The child put her frail arms round the massive shoulders and gave an ineffectual heave.

'Give me my stick,' ordered Mrs Curdle, 'and both your hands!'

With much grunting and moaning she at last struggled to her feet, and stood, swaying slightly, in the gloom.

'Not a word about this to anyone, mind!' said Mrs Curdle, shaking the stick at Rachel.

'All right, Gran,' she whispered.

'Help me back home. Round behind the tents, my dear. Don't want no fuss. It's nothing serious.'

The two made their way into the sunshine. Mrs Curdle leant heavily upon her stick with one hand and rested the other upon Rachel's bony shoulder.

When they reached the caravan Mrs Curdle patted the child's cheek kindly.

'You're a good girl,' she told her. 'Better than your dad, by far. And don't forget – not a word about this. 'Tis only wind round the heart – nothing to worry anyone about.'

She dismissed Rachel with a wave of the stick, hobbled ponderously up the three steps, and sank gratefully upon the bed.

Mrs Curdle lay there very quietly. The sudden nausea which had overcome her had passed away and she was content to let thoughts of Ben, and the future of the fair, flutter through her quiescent mind.

Three o'clock chimed distantly and the sun shone through the caravan door, slanting across the dresser and the money drawer, and throwing Mrs Curdle's bed into deep shade.

She became conscious of furtive footsteps approaching and a shadow fell athwart the money drawer. Mrs Curdle lay very still. There was something menacing, something intensely suspicious, about that motionless shadow. It remained there for a full minute and Mrs Curdle knew that someone waited there, alert and listening, for her movements.

At last she could bear it no longer. Rolling from the bed, she advanced to the door, calling as she went:

'Who's there? What d'you want?'

Outside stood her nephew Sam. His air was unconcerned, but it did not deceive Mrs Curdle. He collected his wits and tried to speak casually.

'Bella says you got such a thing as a inch-tape?' he asked glibly. 'She's making somethin' for the kids.'

Mrs Curdle looked steadily at him, and beneath that hawk-like gaze Sam felt his legs turn to water.

'Tell Bella,' said Mrs Curdle with terrible emphasis, '*when she comes back*, she's already borrowed my inch-tape.'

'Must've forgot,' muttered Sam, backing hastily. 'Thanks, Ma,' he added, and took to his heels.

Mrs Curdle watched him vanish behind the switchback and then turned to the drawer.

'So that's where it's been going,' muttered the old lady to herself grimly. 'And serve me right for leaving it there.'

She opened the drawer, scooped out a note or two and a handful of silver, and stood with it in her hand, gazing at the end of the bed where the Curdle Bank caused a substantial hump at the end of the mattress.

'Can't lift that now,' she told herself, shaking her head ruefully.

She crossed to the mantelpiece, lifted down the pewter teapot, and stuffed the money in with that already stored there. Then very carefully she replaced the teapot and took down the photograph of her smiling son which stood beside it.

'I could do with you now, George, my boy,' she said soberly.

11. Mrs Bailey Visits Neighbours

RUTH BASSETT lay in a deck-chair in the shade of the lime tree which her grandfather had loved.

The afternoon post had brought a letter which lay opened upon her lap. Paul had scooped it joyously from the mat, on his way up to his enforced rest. Ruth had tucked him in and carried the letter to the peaceful garden knowing she would not be interrupted.

But the letter had contained disturbing news. It was from the head of the firm where Ruth worked, and it said:

Dear Miss Bassett,

It seems a long time since you were with us, and I can assure you that we all miss you at the office.

There has to be a certain amount of reorganization in the next few months, and I am writing to know whether we may look forward to your return soon. I need hardly add that we should welcome it, but if you have other plans, I should be glad if you would let me know your decision.

We don't want to hurry you in any way, but naturally we

*should have to advertise for your successor in the unhappy
event of your non-return here, and this should be done
within the next fortnight if we are to get things settled
before June 1st.*

*We all send our best wishes and hope to see you back
among us very soon.*

Well, there it was, thought Ruth, a fair offer that could
not have come at a better time. Now she must make a
decision, and her new-found strength would help her.

She stretched her arms above her head and looked up into
the young leaves above her. Somewhere, high aloft, two
sparrows skirmished among the branches and Ruth wondered if they too had problems to face. Did the siting of a
nest, the choice of building materials, grass, moss, twig, and
feather, perplex those grain-small brains as hers was now
perplexed?

Of one thing she was certain. She could not, under any
circumstances, go back to the office. There would be many
plans to make and they must be made carefully and soon,
but the first step was quite clear. She could not go
back.

At this moment, Ruth heard the click of the garden gate
at the side of the house and saw Mrs Bailey approaching.

She crossed the grass, letter in hand, to meet her.

'You couldn't have come at a better moment,' she cried.
'Come and give me some advice.'

Mrs Bailey looked at Ruth over the top of her reading
glasses. The letter lay upon her lap. She had read it through
twice, with no comment, and now fixed the girl with a
speculative eye.

'And are you going back?' she asked, after a pause.

Ruth wriggled unhappily, making the deck-chair creak

with her movements. A ladybird crawled busily along her bare arm and she bent her worried gaze upon the scarlet speck.

'I hardly know how to tell you,' she said. 'It seems cowardly, I suppose, but – well, somehow I can't.'

Mrs Bailey nodded sympathetically.

'Poor darling,' she said gently. 'Of course, I understand.'

'Oh, don't pity me, for heaven's sake!' burst out Ruth, flinging the ladybird violently from her. 'Or you'll make me cry – and I haven't cried once today! It's really rather a record,' she added, with a crooked smile.

'I wasn't pitying you,' responded Mrs Bailey, with professional briskness. She had had a lifetime's experience with agitated patients and Ruth's tremors did not perturb her unduly. 'At least, not in the way you think. I was just feeling rather sorry that you had such a decision to make so quickly.'

Ruth made no answer for a little while, but picked a grass at her feet and nibbled idly at it. A cuckoo called in the distance, and somewhere, far away, some lambs bleated in the fields beside the Upper Pleshy road.

Their trembling young voices brought back with sharp clarity a picture of that lane which was a favourite walk of Ruth's. Only a few days before she and Paul had wandered between its quickening hedges and trodden the springy grass of the roadside verges, so soon to be miller-white with a froth of cows' parsley and the powdering from a myriad overhanging hawthorn flowers.

It was the thought of the beauty yet to come, the beauty that would flood the countryside in her absence, that tore Ruth's heart. She tried to explain it, in a small apologetic voice, to the doctor's wife.

Mrs Bailey, with her eyes closed against the sunshine, nodded sympathetically.

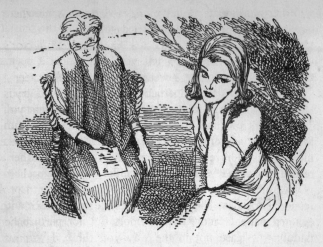

'You see,' finished Ruth, 'it's not so much that I dislike going back to town as finding that I simply cannot bear to leave the country. Joan and I always loved it – but, somehow, since Stephen left me, it has meant much more. More than a lovely place, more than a way of living, and something more than just a comfort. All I know is – I can't do without it now.'

Mrs Bailey did not reply for a minute. She was thinking that, at last, she had heard the girl speak of Stephen. It was the first time that she had said his name, and to hear her talk, calmly and dispassionately, of the absent lover, gave the older woman much satisfaction. There was now no doubt about it. Ruth Bassett's wound had healed.

'Is there any need for you to do without it?' asked Mrs Bailey. 'There must be work in Lulling that you could do. And I know Joan and Edward hope that you will stay here. They have told us so many a time.'

'They've been wonderful,' replied Ruth warmly, 'but I don't feel that I should stay here, in this house, any longer.

But if I could get a tiny flat, or a cottage, somewhere nearby, I believe it would be the answer.'

'I'll keep my eyes and ears open,' promised the doctor's wife. 'Both for posts and somewhere to live.'

She leant forward and placed a hand on the girl's knee.

'You are quite right, and so wise, to see that the country is the only home for you. Some people might think that you are trying to flee from society, that you can't face the fun and fury and stimulus of a crowded life. But I know you better than that.

'Follow your instincts. You've found refreshment here and you'll continue to, I know, for I have too.'

She paused, thinking of that morning's delight in her May garden and her delicious walk down the hill to Lulling while the dew still glittered on Thrush Green. It had taken almost all her life to realize, consciously, how much the country sights and scents around her had contributed to her inner happiness and had provided zest and comfort in turn.

'As one gets older,' she continued slowly, 'so many things get in the way of one's instincts. There's duty to one's children, the necessity to consider a husband's needs and feelings, the knowledge too that one's strength may not be great enough to do what one would like. All sorts of stupid little things too – like wondering what the children would think, or whether a doctor's wife should really do this or that – all these things one considers in relation to a fine, rapturous instinctive desire, and, so often, that fine, rapturous, instinctive desire is gently smothered and its little fire dies under a wet blanket.'

She smiled across at the girl.

'Young people, like you, are much freer. When they see what they want, they cut through difficulties and take it. Just stick by your decision. Make a new life here, and you know that we shall all help you.'

'I'll do that,' promised Ruth gravely. 'When Edward and Joan come back next week we'll talk things over. He offered me a secretarial post in his own firm – and I might begin with that, I think.'

Mrs Bailey smote her substantial thigh a resounding whack.

'Good girl! But do you know what I really came for? To borrow some magazines for poor Ella, and I'd almost forgotten.'

She related the details of Ella's accident, and added that her husband seemed to have realized at last that he must have more help.

'He's resting now,' she said, 'and making very light of his weakness; but he was quite done up when he got back from Dimity's. I thought I'd take Ella something to read. She may turn a page or two and give poor Dimity time to clear up the mess.'

'I'll go and fetch some,' said Ruth, jumping up.

'Not the ordinary women's magazines,' implored Mrs Bailey. 'It's not a bit of good giving love stories to Ella, as you know; but anything with designs and furnishings she'll look at, and even if they only make her blow her top off, it'll keep her attention from her scalds.'

Ruth vanished into the house leaving Mrs Bailey to wander in the warm sunshine of the garden, and to ponder on the girl's vital change.

Now she looked forward, her back turned for ever upon the dark miseries which had held her prisoner for so long.

Mrs Bailey's next visit was to Ella's, and as she crossed Thrush Green, bearing Ruth's carefully-vetted magazines and a bunch of mixed daffodils from the Bassetts' garden, she came face to face with Mrs Curdle.

The old lady was standing by her bright caravan and

Mrs Bailey was shocked at the change in her appearance. Still massive, and still commanding, there was now something pathetic about her. There was a droop about the shoulders and a dullness in those dark eyes which the doctor's wife had not seen before.

The women greeted each other cordially.

'And how are you, Mrs Curdle?'

'Very middlin', ma'am,' answered the old lady. 'Very middlin' indeed. And gets next to no help from my family these days.' She shot a venomous glance in the direction of Sam's caravan.

'But how's your good man?' she continued. 'I hear tell he's been took to his bed for some time past.'

'He's been very poorly, I'm sorry to say,' said Mrs Bailey. 'But improving daily.'

'The years is too much for us,' said Mrs Curdle, with heavy solemnity. She looked across to the doctor's house with a grave face.

'I be coming to see him, after his surgery time, I expect,' went on Mrs Curdle.

'We'll be very pleased to see you,' answered the doctor's wife warmly. 'But he isn't taking surgery at the moment, so just come whenever you can fit it in most conveniently.'

'I'll see the show started, and then be over,' promised Mrs Curdle.

'I hear,' began Mrs Bailey, rather diffidently, 'that you are thinking of retiring. Is it true? We all hope not, you know.'

Mrs Curdle turned a sombre glance upon her.

' 'Tis true I be thinking of it. There's times I feel I can't go on for pain and trouble. But between ourselves, ma'am, I reckons 'twould break my heart to give up.'

She put a dusky hand against the gay paintwork of her caravan, tracing a yellow cut-out leaf, warm in the sunshine.

'Maybe your good man can help me,' went on Mrs Curdle.

'He's been a real friend to me. And you too, ma'am, and that's true.'

'You come and have a word with him,' said Mrs Bailey. 'It'll do him good to see you, I know.'

She made her farewells swiftly, for she did not want to leave her husband alone too long, and Ella had yet to be visited.

But when she had rung Ella's bell and was waiting on the doorstep of the corner cottage, she looked back at the dark figure standing motionless by the gaudy caravan, and felt that she had never seen such loneliness before.

Dimity answered the bell, her hands incarnadined.

'She'll be so pleased to see you,' she twittered, leading the way up the stairs. Mrs Bailey followed her red-speckled legs and scarlet-soled slippers aloft.

Ella Bembridge was an awe-inspiring sight in bed. Her short grey hair stood in a fine shock as she had run her fingers through it in her agitation. A bright red dressing-gown, no less vivid than the dye which bespattered her friend, was pinned at her neck with a gruesome grey monkey's paw, and contrasted strongly with the white bandage which enveloped one scalded hand.

Dimity had erected a tunnel, made with considerable ingenuity, from a bow-fronted fireguard, in order to keep the bedclothes from pressing too heavily upon poor Ella's painful legs, and this great mound, covered with a patchwork quilt of Ella's own making, added to the bizarre effect.

'Nurse is bringing a proper leg-cage later,' said Dimity, gazing with pride at her own handiwork, 'but she's at a baby case at the moment.'

Mrs Bailey admired the present appliance and inquired about the patient's sufferings.

'Simple ruddy torture!' responded Ella with energy. 'If

it hadn't been for your husband I'd have taken a meat-axe to my lower limbs. Couldn't have hurt much more than they do now,' she added, with gloomy relish.

Dimity uttered a horrified squeak.

'Now, darling, don't be so naughty. It'll only make your rash worse.'

'And if you toss about,' warned Mrs Bailey, 'you'll capsize the tunnel.'

'Might just as well give up and die, I suppose,' boomed the patient, with a heartiness that belied her words. 'What about some tea, Dim?'

'Not for me,' said Mrs Bailey hastily, 'I must be getting back. I just wanted to see you and to leave these things.' She put the magazines carefully at Ella's side, well away from the sufferer's hurts, but even so the patient winced away and let out a bellow that set the washstand ringing.

Mrs Bailey tried to look contrite, and Dimity rushed to the bedside.

'Keep back! Keep back!' shouted Ella energetically, like a policeman with an exuberant crowd to control. The two women stood respectfully away from the bed and surveyed the vociferous patient.

'Don't worry,' said Mrs Bailey. 'We'll keep right over here away from your legs. Perhaps I can put these flowers in water for you?'

Dimity hurried away and returned with a large glass jug.

'I can't reach anything else in the kitchen,' she confessed, 'but they should look lovely in that. I must go down again. There's someone at the door.'

She fluttered off again and quietness fell upon the room. Mrs Bailey took the jug and flowers to the washstand, and began to arrange the white and gold daffodils carefully.

Their fragrance crept about the room, adding their breath of spring to the scents and sounds that came through the open window. The rooks wheeled and called above the elms nearby, and from Ella's flower-beds could be heard the chattering and scolding of half a dozen starlings who were busily demolishing her velvety polyanthus flowers. An early bee droned against the pane, his scaly brown legs tap-tapping against the glass like the frail twigs of the jasmine nearby.

Ella watched, in one of her rare silences, as Mrs Bailey moved the blossoms, standing back every now and again to survey her handiwork. The glass jug had been a happy choice, for the soft green beauty of the stalks and leaves could be seen. A myriad tiny air bubbles studded their length, like crystal beads, and Ella, whose gruff exterior hid a discerning sensitivity to loveliness, was moved to speak.

'They're perfect, Winnie. Don't muck 'em about any more. They're just absolutely right in that jug.'

'Clever of Dimity to get it,' murmured Mrs Bailey, still engrossed.

'I must say,' went on Ella, now emerged from her brief spell of quietness, 'it's a real pleasure to see flowers allowed to arrange themselves comfortably against the side of a vase, instead of being threaded through an entanglement of squashed-up chicken wire, or that wadding stuff the Lulling Floral Club will foist on its members.'

'Oh, come,' protested Mrs Bailey, advancing upon Ella with a pheasant-eye narcissus flower which had broken off. 'I think you must have some help sometimes for flowers. Think of nasturtiums or cowslips!'

She held out the flower to Ella to smell, but she made such violent gestures of dismissal, rocking the fireguard perilously, that Mrs Bailey tossed her the flower and returned to the washstand. Ella raised the blossom to her heated face and continued her harangue between violent sniffs at its snowy petals.

'Well, I've got no time for the Floral Club, as I've told you all before. It doesn't matter which house you go into within a radius of six miles, you can always tell if the mistress goes to the Lulling meetings.' She flung a bolster-like arm in the direction of Mrs Bailey and pointed an accusing finger at her.

'You know what I mean. You do it yourself. *April!* Everybody's got some prissy little workbox fished out from the attic and stuffed up with primroses and moss. *May!* Dam' great boughs of cherry blossom, impaled on wire, and perched up above eye-level somewhere where they're bound to get blown down. *June!* One iris, Japanese fashion, in a "cool-grey" or "celadon-green" vase!'

Mrs Bailey, shaking with laughter at her friend's vehemence, tried to protest, but was brushed aside.

'*July!*' continued Ella, warming to her theme. 'Three gladioli in a horrible flat white object, and arranged like a one-masted barque, with one up in the middle, and the other two horizontally fore and aft! And as for Christmas –'

Ella took a large breath, and turned a reddening, ferocious face upon her convulsed friend.

'I tell you plainly – now, in ample time. If you're thinking of concocting some horrible great table decoration out of plastic fern, dried grass, two dusty old sprigs of left-over Cape gooseberries, some ghastly artificial flowers from the haberdasher's, topped up with the bunch of violets you've worn to Lulling funerals for the past ten years, plus three poor little Roman hyacinths – like waifs among the corpses – then you can think again! I can face up to silver-painted holly, if that's what you people have in mind, with the rest of you – but I'm damned if I'll thank anybody, even you, Winnie dear, for a monstrosity like that. Or for an armful of frosted beetroot leaves!'

'Darling,' said Mrs Bailey, wiping her eyes, 'I promise

you that I'll give you nothing floral at all when Christmas comes.'

She bent towards her old friend and gently kissed her good-bye.

Ella, her spirits as much restored by her own loquacity as by the flowers and the company, beamed her farewells. She had stuck the narcissus behind one ear, like a Pacific Island maiden. Its fragility contrasted strongly with the weather-beaten cheek against which it fell, and gave an added rakishness to her raffish appearance.

A large tabby cat, which was the adored pet of the house, crept in as Mrs Bailey opened the bedroom door. It glided to the bedside, gathered itself together, and leapt heavily upon its mistress's lap. Mrs Bailey, who had been powerless to forestall it, waited for screams and imprecations to rend the air. None came.

'Dear old puss,' cooed Ella lovingly, enveloping the creature in an embrace of red dressing-gown. 'Come to see your poor old mum, have you?'

Mrs Bailey closed the door quietly upon their reunion, and crept downstairs. At least, she told herself with amusement, she could let her husband know that one patient was well on the way to recovery.

12. A Family Fight

CURDLE'S Fair was now in readiness for its grand opening, soon after six, in about two hours' time.

It was not a large fair, it is true, but to its owner and its admirers in Thrush Green and dozens of other villages scattered across half a dozen counties, it had everything that was essential for an evening of delicious noise and heady vertigo.

The roundabout was the centre-piece. Its brass winked in the sunshine, and the dappled horses, legs stretched and nostrils aflare, galloped in eternal fury. A switchback, a trifle shabby about its red plush seats, but capable of dizzy speed, stood nearby; while eight swing-boats, painted red and blue, provided more sensation, and hung now, idly swaying beneath the striped furry sallies of their ropes. Later, as darkness fell, the youths of Lulling would tug with sweating palms at those hairy grips, vying with each other for speed and height and causing their terrified passengers to scream with mingled fear and ecstasy. What could be more exhilarating than the music of those faint screams, tribute to one's manly strength, added to the wild rush of night air as the boat swept up and back in a breath-taking arc, with the glare of the fair's lights swirling below and the pale stars glimmering above? The swing-boats were rarely idle once the fair began, but now, in the heat of the afternoon, they seemed to drowse, like boats at anchor in some serene harbour, swaying gently, in that lovelier element than water, above the rippling green grass.

The marquee that housed the menagerie was now in readiness. Rachel, shaken but obediently silent, had finished her ministrations there and now sat plaiting her hair on the steps of her home.

The coconuts stood poised upon the red-and-white striped posts that Ben had rammed home that morning. Five or six stalls – rolling pennies into a square, toy ducks to be caught with a magnet, the wheel of fortune, and the like – awaited their customers. Above each stall, festooned against a glitter of mirrors, hung teddy bears, dolls, teapots, cushions, kettles, crockery, watches, knives, and a host of prizes to dazzle covetous eyes.

A shooting range, with playing cards pricked with a thousand pin-marks, displayed similar prizes and some of a humbler type, pottery figures of dogs, gnomes, and unsteady baskets, doomed to break, chip, and peel in less than no time and to find a merciful end in a cottage dustbin.

A few small booths completed the fair. Some old sweets, great humbugs as big as a child's fist, vast flat tins of treacle toffee that cracked beneath the stallholder's metal hammer like brown enchanted glass, and billowing clouds of pink-and-white candy floss. Hanging at the side of one stall from a great hook, was a wonderful silky skein of sweet sugar floss which was pulled and twisted, looped and tossed, by dusky hands which were a seven-day wonder to the open-mouthed children and a shocking affront to their elders.

Two of the smaller booths flashed like Aladdin's cave with a galaxy of cheap jewellery. It was from one of these that Molly's much-loved cornflower brooch had come. Bracelets, necklaces, ear-rings, powder cases, and jewelled pins for scarf and hair sparkled with rubies, sapphires, diamonds, emeralds, pearls, and topazes, no less dazzling because they were of glass. They twinkled in the brilliant sunshine, reflecting its light from a thousand facets. Later they would flash even more brightly beneath the harsh lights set against the mirrored roof above them.

They expressed the very essence of the fair, garish but gay, seductive but innocent, phoney but fascinating.

And in many a cottage home next day, one of those sparkling trinkets would be treasured as the souvenir of an enchanted evening, when hearts were as young and light as the newly broken leaves that whispered on Thrush Green's trees.

The infants had already straggled out of school. They had sung their grace, led by Miss Fogerty's quavering soprano :

'Thank you for the world so sweet.
Thank you for the food we eat.
Thank you for the birds that sing,
Thank you, God, for everything.'

Some were sharp, some flat, some growled tunelessly, but all took it along at a spanking pace, determined to get out into the exciting canvas world of the fair, which had sprung up so miraculously since morning.

Shouting, running, trailing coats too hot to wear on this golden afternoon, they had vanished from Miss Fogerty's sight.

Sighing with exhaustion the teacher bent down and loosened her shoelaces. There was nothing more tiring to the feet than a sudden burst of warm weather, she told herself. Tomorrow, if it lasted, she decided, as she locked her desk and swept the snippets of coloured paper which littered it into the waste-paper basket, she really must look out her Clarks' sandals and be comfortable.

At the same time Molly and Ben were descending the steep path through Lulling Woods on their way to Thrush Green.

The laundry van had called early, and Ben had persuaded Molly that the main reason for lingering at The Drovers' Arms had now vanished.

'Give us the chicken food,' he had directed, 'and I'll chuck it over while you tidies up.'

'But what about my missus?' Molly had said, pretending to be anxious.

'Leave her a note. You can write, can't you?' he said, with a wry smile. Molly gave him a sudden hug, delighted that he could now joke about something that had worried him so recently. The hug was returned warmly, and would have been prolonged indefinitely had not Molly broken away, thrust the chicken's bucket into her lover's hand, and run upstairs to put on the yellow spotted frock and hair ribbon.

Within half an hour they had emerged from the cool greenery of the woods into the golden meadows below. They walked slowly, arms round each other's waist, stopping every few paces to kiss or gaze with wonder at each other. After a year of doubt, loneliness, and despair the sudden revelation of their true feelings overwhelmed them. They were in the grip of the age-old spell of first love, and moved like beings entranced.

Ben had never felt so buoyant, so confident, and so invulnerable before. All the world was his, and there was nothing that he could not attempt now that he knew Molly was his.

But Molly, despite her happiness, felt apprehensive about the meeting with old Mrs Curdle. She had been a figure of awe-inspiring majesty to the girl all her life, and the thought of those black eyes scrutinizing and criticizing her was indeed a fearsome one.

'I could give you a cup of tea at our house,' she said shyly. 'The key's under the mat, and you'll have to meet my dad some time.'

'I daresay,' answered Ben, stopping again and holding his girl at arms' length. He knew all that was passing in her mind and laughed aloud to think that she should fear to meet old Gran.

'But I'm taking you straight to Gran's, and she'll give you more than a cup of tea. She'll give you the biggest welcome you've ever had. You'll see, she'll be that pleased!' promised young Ben earnestly, and Molly took what comfort she could from his assurances.

It was at this moment that they became conscious of a distant voice calling to them. Dotty Harmer, at the end of her garden, one hand clamping the enormous sun hat to her head and the other holding up a basket, was trying to attract their attention. They left the dusty path and waded through the sea of buttercups to her hedge, Molly hastily detaching herself from her companion's grasp.

'You wait here,' she urged. 'I won't be a minute.'

She approached the low hedge.

'Good afternoon, Miss Harmer,' she said demurely.

'Molly, be a good girl and take these few things in to Miss Bembridge. Have you heard about her accident?'

'No, indeed!' exclaimed Molly, and listened to the tale. She took the basket and lifted it over the hedge. Inside were various bottles and jars huddled under a dishevelled bunch of wilting primroses.

'I can't get up to Thrush Green myself,' went on Dotty, speaking of the place as though it were in another hemisphere, 'as the cat's kittening and she does like a little support at these times.'

She cast an inquisitive glance at the distant Ben.

'And who is the young man?' she inquired.

Curious old cat, thought Molly rebelliously, why should I tell her? But Miss Harmer, despite her scarecrow appearance, still occasioned a vestige of respect and a certain amount of pity too, so that the girl answered civilly.

'He's Ben Curdle, from the fair.'

The sound of anguished mewing floated from the shed nearby and Dotty turned away hastily.

'Many thanks,' she called as she went. 'Just drop it in, Molly.'

She vanished from sight and Molly rejoined Ben.

'She potty?' inquired the young man, nodding towards the cottage.

'Not really,' replied Molly tolerantly. 'Just had too much book learning.'

Together they resumed their interrupted progress to Thrush Green.

Meanwhile, Sam bit his nails and sat, glowering, on the steps of his caravan. The heat of the day and his own black temper caused him to sweat profusely. He untied his gaudy neckerchief and threw it behind him on to the floor of the caravan.

Well, that put paid to the horses for the afternoon, he told himself morosely. The old girl was back in the caravan and not likely to budge again. He remembered the cold, glittering look which she had cast him and Sam's craven soul shuddered at the remembrance.

The church clock chimed the first quarter, the silvery sound floating down through the sunny air as lightly as the summer insects that made the air murmurous about him. In fifteen minutes, thought Sam savagely, Rougemont would be setting off to win – and not a penny would he have on him.

He leapt to his feet, unable to sit still any longer under such provocation, and prowled behind the canvas enclosure of Ben's coconut shies. It was very quiet.

Not a soul was in sight, although he could hear the voices of women in a neighbouring caravan and the cries of the school children making their way home across Thrush Green.

At that moment he saw Mrs Curdle. She descended the steps of her caravan and made her way steadily in the direction of the menagerie tent. The old lady was about to continue her disturbed inspection. Sam noticed how heavily she leant upon her ebony stick, but it was not pity which moved his heart. A searing flash of hope caused it to throb. Talk of luck, he told himself! There still might be a chance!

His fears forgotten in the excitement of a flutter and a

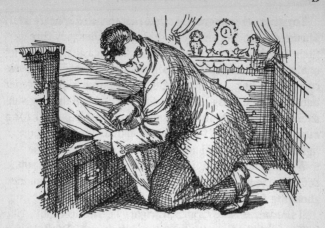

race against time, Sam moved swiftly towards the caravan. Its doorway faced away from the centre of the fair and he entered unobserved.

He wasted no time in investigating the drawer or the teapot, but crept to the end of Mrs Curdle's bed and heaved frantically at the mattress which enveloped the Curdle Bank.

Ben and Molly approached Mrs Curdle's caravan from the rear.

Molly had delivered Dotty's basket into Dimity's hands, had received her profuse thanks, and had inquired with real sympathy after poor Miss Bembridge. Molly had received many kindnesses from both ladies and felt for them affection mingled with some pity for their maiden state.

Her errand done, she returned to Ben with a fluttering heart, for now the time had come to face his formidable grandparent.

'Oh, Ben,' she said, suddenly faltering on the verge of Thrush Green, and turning beseeching eyes upon him.

Ben gave her that crinkly smile that turned her heart over, squeezed her hand, and said nothing. Together they threaded their way behind the booths and stalls, occasionally passing one of the Curdle tribe who glanced interestedly at Ben's companion but said nothing. Only a fair-girl, feeding her baby, and humming blissfully to herself in the drowsy sunshine, nodded to Molly and smiled at Ben. He paused for a moment to chirrup to the child and to flick his cousin's light hair, but they did not speak.

As they neared the caravan they could hear the sound of movement inside. Ben stopped, arrested by a sudden thought.

'I best make sure Gran's all right,' he said to Molly. 'She has a laydown sometimes of an afternoon. Wait half a minute for me.'

Molly nodded so eagerly and thankfully at this brief reprieve that Ben, now that no eyes were upon them, gave her a swift fierce hug and kiss that left her breathless.

Still laughing, he left her standing in the sunshine and ran lightly round the caravan and up the steps.

The scene that met Ben's astonished gaze needed no explanation. After the dazzle outside, the interior of Mrs Curdle's caravan was murky, but Ben saw enough to justify his swift action.

The bunk bed lay tumbled, and upon the crumpled quilt was the Curdle Bank. The lid of the battered case was open, displaying a muddle of banknotes and silver and copper coins.

Sam, on being disturbed, had cowered as far as he could into a corner by the glittering stove. One hand he held up as if to ward off a blow, and the other was hidden behind his back.

His eyes were terrified as he gazed at the intruder who

barred his only way of escape. His mouth dropped open, and a few incoherent bubbling sounds were the nearest that he could get to speech. Not that he was given time to account for himself, for Ben was upon him in a split second, gripping his arms painfully.

Sam twisted and heaved this way and that, trying to hide the notes in his hand, but Ben jerked his arm viciously behind him, and turned him inexorably towards the light. The notes fluttered to the floor.

Ben gave a low animal growl of fury and Sam a shrill scream of sudden pain. He lunged sharply with his knee. The two men parted for a moment, then turned face to face, and locked in a terrible panting embrace began to wrestle, one desperate with fear and the other afire with fury.

They lurched and thudded this way and that within the narrow confines of Mrs Curdle's home. Ben's shoulder brought down half a dozen plates from the diminutive dresser. Sam's foot jerked a saucepan from the hob, and the hissing water added its sound to the clamour which grew as the fight grew more vicious.

Molly, aghast at the noise, ran to see what was happening and, appalled at the sight, fled to get help. The flaxen-haired girl, still holding the baby to her breast, was wandering towards her.

'It's a fight!' gasped Molly. The girl looked mildly surprised, but uttered no word, merely continuing in an unhurried manner, to approach the source of the uproar.

Molly ran round a stall and was amazed to see a number of the Curdles converging rapidly upon her. There were about a dozen altogether, including several young children, whose eyes were alight with pleasurable anticipation at the thought of witnessing a fight.

The bush telegraph of the fairground was in action. These first spectators hurried past Molly, and, in the distance, she could see others, jumping down the steps of their caravans, calling joyously to each other of this unlooked-for excitement and scurrying to swell the crowd which was fast collecting round Mrs Curdle's caravan.

Emerging from one of the tents Molly saw the great lady herself. A small fair-haired girl tugged agitatedly at her hand, urging her to hurry. The old lady's face was grim. She bore down upon the shrinking Molly like some majestic ship, and passed her without even noticing the trembling girl.

Emboldened by the example of this dominating head of the tribe, Molly braced herself, and like a small dinghy following in the wake of a liner she crept after Ben's grandmother and back to the scene of battle.

The spectators who had been vociferous, quietened as their leader stalked into their midst.

It was a tense moment. Ben had forced Sam to the doorway and they grappled and swayed dangerously at the head of the steps. They made a wild and terrifying sight, bloodied and dishevelled.

There was a sudden convulsive movement, a sickening crack as Sam's jaw and Ben's bony fist met, and Sam fell bodily backwards to the grass. He rolled over, scattering some of the crowd, groaned, twitched, and lay still.

A great sigh rippled round the onlookers, like the sound of wind through corn, and Mrs Curdle strode to the foot of the steps. She spared no glance for the prostrate man at her feet, but looked unblinkingly at Ben, who swayed, bruised, and dizzy, against the door frame. A trickle of blood ran across his swelling cheek, and blood dripped from his broken knuckles upon the dusty black corduroy trousers.

Nobody watching the old lady could guess her feelings. Her dusky face was inscrutable, her mouth pressed into a hard thin line. Ben looked down upon her forlornly and broke the heavy silence.

'He asked for it, Gran,' he said apologetically.

Mrs Curdle made no sign, but her heart melted at the words. Just so, she remembered, had George looked, so many, many years ago, when she had caught him fighting another six-year-old. He too had swayed on his feet, and had looked outwardly contrite, whilst all the time, as she very well knew, he had secretly gloried in his victory. The sudden memory stabbed her so sharply, and filled her with such mingled sorrow and pride, that she continued to gaze at George's son (who might be George himself, so dearly did she love him) in utter silence.

Ben's eyes met his grandmother's and in that long shared look he knew what lay in her heart. He had proved himself; and to that love which she had always borne him another quality had been added. It was reliance upon him, and Ben rejoiced that it was so.

'Gran!' he cried, descending the steps with his arms outstretched. But the old lady shook her head and turned to face the crowd. And Ben, content with his new knowledge, waited patiently behind her.

It was at this moment that Bella and her three children came upon the scene. She had been told the news as she struggled up the hill from Lulling, and now arrived, screaming, breathless, and blaspheming, her yellow hair streaming in the breeze, like some vengeful harpy. At the sound of her voice, Sam groaned, and struggled into a sitting posture, his aching head supported by his battered fists.

Mrs Curdle raised her ebony stick and Bella's torrent of abuse slowed down. Beneath the old lady's black implacable silence she gradually faltered to a stop, and began to weep instead, the three children adding their wails to their mother's.

At last the old lady spoke, and those who heard her never forgot those doom-laden words. Thunder should have rolled and lightning flashed as Mrs Curdle drew herself up to her great height, and, pointing the ebony stick at Sam, spoke his sentence.

'You and yours,' she said slowly, each word dropping like a cold stone, 'go from here tomorrow. And never, never come back!'

She turned her solemn gaze upon the gaping crowd, and, with a flick of the ebony stick, dismissed them. Two men assisted Sam to his feet and amidst lamentations from his family he hobbled to his caravan.

Mrs Curdle watched the rest of the tribe melt away and turned to question Ben at the foot of the steps.

But Ben was not there. She looked sharply about trying to catch sight of him among the departing spectators and suddenly saw him. He was some distance off, talking earnestly to a pretty young girl, beneath a tree.

As Mrs Curdle watched, she saw him take the girl's hand. They advanced towards her, the girl looking shy and hanging back. But there was nothing shy about Ben, thought Mrs Curdle, shaken with secret laughter and loving pride.

For, bruised and bloody, torn and dusty as he was, Ben radiated supreme happiness as he limped towards her across Thrush Green; and Mrs Curdle rejoiced with him.

PART THREE *Night*

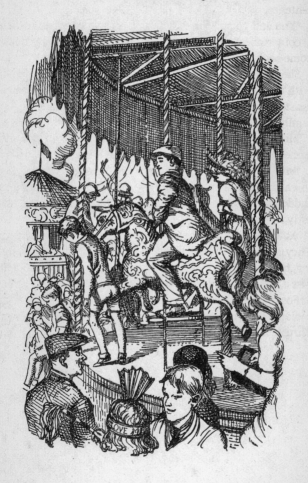

13. Music on Thrush Green

THE sun was beginning to dip its slow way downhill to hide, at last, behind the dark mass of Lulling Woods.

The streets of Lulling still kept their warmth, and the mellow Cotswold stone of the houses glowed like amber as the rays of the sun deepened from gold to copper.

On Thrush Green the chestnut trees sloped their shadows towards Doctor Bailey's house. The great bulk of the church was now in the shade, crouching low against the earth like a massive mother hen. But the weathercock on St Andrew's lofty steeple still gleamed against the clear sky, and from his perch could see the River Pleshy far below, winding its somnolent way between the water meadows and reflecting the willows and the drinking cattle which decorated its banks.

Although twilight had not yet come the lights of the fair were switched on at a quarter past six, and the first strains of music from the roundabout spread the news that Mrs Curdle's annual fair was now open.

The news was received, by those who heard it on Thrush Green, in a variety of ways. Sour old Mr Piggott, who had looked in at St Andrew's to make sure that all was in readiness for the two churchings at six-thirty, let fall an ejaculation, quite unsuitable to its surroundings, and, emerging from the vestry door, crunched purposefully and maliciously upon a piece of coke to relieve his feelings.

Ella Bembridge, who had eaten a surprisingly substantial tea for one suffering from burns, shock, and a rash, groaned aloud and begged Dimity to close the window against 'that benighted hullabaloo'. Dimity had done so and had removed the patient's empty tray, noting with satisfaction that she had finished the small pot of quince jelly sent by Dotty Harmer that afternoon. In the press of events, she had omitted to tell Ella of Dotty's kindness, and now, seeing the inroads that her friend had made into Dotty's handiwork, she decided not to mention it. Ella could be so very scathing about Dotty's cooking, thought Dimity, descending the crooked stairs, but obviously the quince jelly had been appreciated.

Paul, beside himself with excitement, was leaping up and down the hall, singing at the top of his voice. Occasionally he broke off to bound up to Ruth's bedroom where she was getting ready. The appalling slowness with which she arranged her hair and powdered her face, drove her small nephew almost frantic. This was the moment he had been waiting for all day – for weeks – for a whole year! Would she *never* be ready?

To young Doctor Lovell, returning from a visit to Upper Pleshy in his shabby two-seater, the colour and glitter of the fair offered a spectacle of charming innocence. Here was yet another aspect of Thrush Green to increase his growing affection for the place. Throughout the day he had found himself thinking of his happiness in this satisfying practice. He could settle here so easily, he told himself, slipping into place among the friendly people of Lulling, enjoying their company and sharing their enchanting countryside.

He drew up outside Doctor Bailey's house, and, resting his arms across the steering wheel, watched the bright scene with deep pleasure. This was the first time he had seen Mrs Curdle's fair. It would probably be the only time, he told himself grimly, for Mrs Curdle might not return next year, and if she did, who was to know where he would be?

The thought was so painful that Doctor Lovell jerked his

long legs out of the car, slammed the door, and moved swiftly towards the surgery to find solace in his work.

Mrs Bailey heard the familiar noise of the surgery door, and looked over the top of her spectacles, just in time to see young Doctor Lovell vanish inside.

She was sitting in the window seat, sewing, and enjoying the last rays of the sunshine which had transfigured the whole day.

Doctor Bailey lay comfortably on the couch attempting to solve *The Times* crossword which lay upon his bony knees. He had recovered from his afternoon's bout of weakness and, to his wife's discerning eye, he appeared more serene and confident than he had for many weeks – as indeed he was. For having resolved to offer young Lovell a partnership in the practice his mind was at rest. That agonizing spasm in the brilliant sunshine of Thrush Green had taught him a sharp lesson and he was a wise enough man to heed it.

His decision made, at terms with himself and the world, the old doctor was content to let his body and mind relax, awaiting the end of surgery hours when he could put his proposal to his new young helper. That he would accept it, Doctor Bailey had no doubt at all.

The room had been quiet, with that companionable silence born of mutual ease. When the music of the fair blared out it made no difference to the peace of the two listeners. It was the first of May on Thrush Green, and music was its right and fitting accompaniment.

It was also the overture to Mrs Curdle's annual visit, remembered Mrs Bailey. She let her needlework drop into her lap and looked at last year's bunch of wood-shaving flowers which she had conscientiously put into a tall vase ready for Mrs Curdle's polite inspection later.

Her mind flew back to her first view of young Mrs Curdle, with baby George securely fastened to her hip by an enveloping bright shawl, holding the first of many mammoth bouquets. Poor George, thought Mrs Bailey, so loved, so dear, so soon to leave his adoring mother to be killed in battle. What a tragic loss, not only for inconsolable Mrs Curdle, but for their fair and, for that matter, the country as a whole.

Mrs Bailey's thoughts slipped back, as they so often did, to those lost young friends of both wars, and she wondered, yet again, if the world would have been different had they lived. It would have been enriched, of that she had no doubt, for all those lives had something of value – some facet of truth and beauty – to offer, that would have illumined other men's lives as well as their own. The world we must accept as it is, she recognized that fact philosophically, but it did not stop one from pondering on its limitless possibilities if those others, untimely dead, had had their way with it.

Her husband's voice recalled Mrs Bailey from 'old unhappy, far-off things, and battles long ago' to the present.

'Dairycats,' he was saying speculatively. 'An anagram. Any idea?'

'Caryatids,' responded Mrs Bailey, without hesitation. Beaming, the doctor filled in the clue in his neat precise hand. Now that the spell of silence was broken Mrs Bailey told her husband about her meeting before tea with old Mrs Curdle.

'And she looks quite desperately ill,' she said. 'And as far as I could gather, she wants to consult you. I did hint gently that Doctor Lovell would be taking the surgery tonight –'

'She won't take that hint!' pronounced Doctor Baily emphatically. 'In any case, I should like to see her myself, and I don't think she would allow anyone else to examine her.'

'Well, I certainly hope you'll find her fit to carry on,' said Mrs Bailey. 'I can't imagine May the first without that background!'

She nodded her head in time with the raucous and distorted rendering of 'Happy Days are Here Again' which floated through the open window.

'She'll keep going if there's half a chance,' prophesied the doctor. 'She's a grand old girl. She won't want to give up any more than I do.'

He wriggled himself into a more comfortable position, then wagged a solemn finger at his wife.

'You know what? Mrs Curdle and I are in the same boat. We're old and we don't like it. I think we shall both feel better when we've faced that uncomfortable fact. Now, my dear, give me your advice. Should you say that "Knickerbocker Glory" was an anagram?'

Across the road, on Thrush Green itself, the head of the fair moved methodically from one stall to the next. Mrs Curdle's dark eyes missed nothing, and as the members of her tribe saw her approach they straightened up the prizes, flicked the dust from mirrors and brass, and renewed their shouts of encouragement to the few customers already exploring the attractions.

Tonight, particularly, after the scene of Sam's shame, her family were on the qui vive. Ma, on the war path, was a figure they had cause to fear, and this was pay day too. Curdle's Fair was at its most efficient.

Sam was at his post, by the switchback, despite a bruised face, a swollen jaw containing two loose teeth, and a headache which normally would have kept him in his bunk bed.

He knew well enough that he would have more to suffer if Mrs Curdle found him malingering on his last day in her employ.

Bella, to his amazement, had said little, too confounded by the shock of dismissal and Sam's disgrace to remonstrate further. She had, often enough, he remembered bitterly, nagged him to leave the fair. Well, now he had no option but to go. He leant his aching back against the painted support of the switchback, his dizzy head whirling as madly and as noisily as the machinery behind him. It said much for Mrs Curdle's discipline that Sam never for one moment considered approaching her for forgiveness or change of heart. From that implacable matriarch nothing, he knew, would be gained. Go he must, and in the early light of dawn, when Mrs Curdle's retinue took the high road towards the north, on its way to join a large fair at an ancient market town near Oxford, Sam's family would be missing from the procession. He knew, from experience of other family outcasts from the Curdle tribe, that he would never be spoken of again.

He straightened up as he saw the old lady bearing down upon him. She looked better than she had done all day. She carried the ebony stick, but leant upon it less obviously, and her flashing eyes above the jutting haughty nose had a fire in them which had been missing for many a long day. It was as if the fight had given her new strength. Many a woman, the victim of robbery and treachery in her own family, would have been shaken with shock, but Mrs Curdle was made of lusty stuff and had thrived all her life on just such battles. Firmly she approached the switchback and the trembling, unhappy Sam.

She gave a grim searching glance at the circling contraption, her hawk gaze passing over her nephew without a flicker. He might have been one of the gnats that hovered in her path, so little notice did she take of him. Neither by word nor gesture did she acknowledge his presence. He was no longer part of Mrs Curdle's world.

She passed on, leaving Sam even more wretched than before. The thought of a drink at The Two Pheasants floated ravishingly into Sam's dizzy head, and was instantly rejected. Sam knew when he was beaten, and watched this tyrant continue her regal progress towards the coconut shies, where Ben, with Molly beside him, exhorted the customers to greater efforts.

And, to his chagrin, Sam saw the old lady's grim mouth soften into a warm smile as she approached the pair.

It had been an extraordinary tea party in Mrs Curdle's caravan that afternoon, and Molly was never to forget it.

When Sam had departed, and the crowd had vanished as quickly as it had formed, Ben had found her half-way home. Already under considerable strain from the emotion of the day, and strung up at the thought of meeting Ben's formidable grandmother, poor Molly had found this sudden, fierce, silent fight absolutely unbearable. She had determined to slip back to the cottage and to venture forth later when the rumpus had died down.

Ben, bleeding and dishevelled, was a fearsome figure when he caught up with her, but his dark eyes shone and his voice was gentle as he pleaded with her to return with him. She could not refuse him and he had led her back to that awe-inspiring figure at the foot of the caravan steps. Mrs Curdle had watched in silence as they approached and it was Ben who spoke first.

'Gran, this is Molly. She lives over the green. I've brought her to tea.' He wiped a hand across his cheek, and looked with some surprise at the blood on his fingers.

Mrs Curdle turned a smile upon the girl, so quick, so warm, and so like Ben's that Molly's fears fell from her.

'You be very welcome,' said the old lady, graciously,

inclining her head with a royal gesture. She turned to Ben, who stood beaming upon them both.

'And if you be coming to tea too you'd best wash that muck off yourself,' she ordered. Ben pulled himself together and began to brush the dust from his corduroy trousers.

'I'll get cleaned up, Gran,' he promised and set off towards his caravan. Mrs Curdle watched him go with a smile.

'He's a good boy,' she murmured, as if to herself. 'A real good boy. His dad all over again.'

For a moment she seemed to have forgotten Molly and to have slipped away to some time or place of which the girl knew nothing. But, after a long minute, she sighed and turned politely to her guest.

'Come you in, my dear. And if we're going to get a cup of tea – well, maybe you'll give me a hand tidying up the mess them young fellows have made.'

The two women had mounted the steps and faced the turmoil. Molly was used to creating order from chaos and wasted no time on useless bewailing. Old Mrs Curdle sat on the edge of her tumbled bed and began returning the scattered money to the attaché case, whilst the girl swept up broken china, replaced the pots and pans that littered the floor, and mopped up the water that had been spilt round Mrs Curdle's shining stove. The old lady watched her deft movements with approval.

'You known my Ben long?' she inquired shrewdly.

'Since last year,' said Molly, looking up from her mopping. She wrung out a dripping cloth into an enamel bowl and set to again. It was easier to talk with her hands occupied in such familiar tasks and her qualms were leaving her under the kindly scrutiny of the old lady on the bed.

'He's a boy you can trust,' Mrs Curdle said soberly. 'No fly-by-night, young Ben. But he wouldn't stand for any flirting, mind!'

Molly flushed.

'There's no need for him to,' she retorted. 'I ain't the flirting kind.' The thought of her year's unhappy vigil pricked her into speech again, for the old lady's words rankled.

'I been waiting to hear from him for a twelve-month, and refused a-plenty, and that's flat!'

She rubbed energetically at a tarnished streak on the side of the stove. Her mouth was rebellious and Mrs Curdle stretched down a dusky hand to the curly head that bobbed so near her knee.

'You don't need to take on, my dear,' said Mrs Curdle very gently. 'Ben won't look at no one else. And I hope – yes, I do hope – as you'll see fit to stick to our Ben. You're the one for him.'

The girl sat back on her heels, still clutching the wet cloth, and the two women exchanged a look of complete understanding. Mutual affection, respect, and the love which they both bore Ben united them in that instant. The bond was never to be broken.

'How old be you?' asked Mrs Curdle, resuming her tidying.

'Near enough eighteen,' answered Molly, rising to her feet. She rested the enamel bowl easily against her hip and old Mrs Curdle looked her up and down approvingly.

'I had my first at eighteen,' said she, nodding sagely. ' 'Tis a good thing to start a family young in our line of business. They helps as you gets older and the big 'uns brings on the little 'uns.'

Molly was momentarily disconcerted at this calm acceptance of the position.

'My dad don't know nothing about Ben. I keeps house for him really. He'll have something to say if I tell him.'

'Ben'll call on your dad tonight,' pronounced Mrs Curdle

finally. 'There's no call to be flustered. I don't doubt Ben'd rush you off to church tomorrow if he had his way. Ben's always hasty, and his dad was the same, But, at eighteen, going steady's no crime for a bonny girl like you, and your dad can like it or lump it.'

'He won't like it, that I do know,' said Molly emphatically. 'He don't like travelling people. He'll say I'm –' She hesitated, anxious not to hurt the old lady's feelings by putting the ordinary settled man's suspicions of the nomad into words.

Mrs Curdle gazed at her shrewdly.

'He'll say you're throwing yourself away on a gipsy, who ain't got two ha'pennies to rub together. Is that it?'

The girl nodded unhappily. There was a silence in the little caravan, broken only by the fluttering of an early butterfly against the sunny caravan window.

'Do you think you are?' asked the old lady at length. The girl's face lit up.

'Never!' she said softly. Mrs Curdle sighed happily.

'There's time for your dad to get used to the idea of your marrying a gipsy boy. Won't hurt you two to wait a few months and start your married life when we're resting for the winter. And besides –'

She paused as though wondering if she should add what was in her mind. The girl waited, with her head on one side, looking down at that dark thoughtful face.

'And besides,' continued Mrs Curdle, 'what your dad don't know is that Ben's no pauper, but a chap with a grand business behind him. He needn't fear his daughter'll starve while Curdle's Fair is going strong.'

At that moment, Ben had appeared in the doorway, washed and clad in clean clothing.

'Ain't you two women had time to put the kettle on with all that talking?' he inquired. And grabbing the empty vessel from the side of the hob he went, whistling, to remedy their omission.

And now, as the sunset did its best to rival the gaudy splendour of the fair, Mrs Curdle finished the tour of her little world with her spirits restored. Every booth and side-show and every piece of machinery was in order and buckling to its daily business. The clamour, the shouting, the throbbing of motors, and the oily smell that emanated from them and was as incense in the nostrils of the old lady who owned them, filled the warm evening air.

Up the steep hill from Lulling in the south, across the western golden meadows below Lulling Woods and down from the north-lying hamlets of Upper Pleshy, Nod, and Nidden, came the country folk to enjoy the brief pleasures of the glittering fair.

For tonight Thrush Green throbbed and beat like a great heart, pulsing out its message to the countryside around, and there were many who answered the call, remembering, with a pang, that it might be the last time that they would hear it.

With a heart as bright and indomitable as the fair itself Mrs Curdle stood at the doorway of her home and surveyed the bustle. It had been a good day, she told herself, trash thrown out and a bit of real gold found, she fancied, thinking of Ben's fine girl. Well, there it was, her fair, her whole world, spinning away as usual, and quite capable of looking after itself for an hour or two while she took time off to face the last job of this long, bright day!

She turned her back upon it resolutely and began to prepare herself for her visit to Doctor Bailey.

14. All the Fun of the Fair

PAUL'S happiness was complete. At last he was in the midst of that glorious world which he had seen being created, that morning, from his bedroom window. It was even more intoxicating than he had remembered it. Were there ever such lights, such music, and such a galaxy of pleasures?

He gripped his aunt's hand, but was unconscious of her presence. His eyes and mouth formed three great O's, and he was oblivious of everything but the splendour which surrounded him. His school-fellows hailed him, grown-up friends spoke to him, but he was too entranced to notice them. This was a magic world and he was in its spell.

Ruth led him towards the roundabout, for she knew that this was his favourite attraction of the fair. He clambered up the steep wooden step and edged purposefully towards an ostrich, a creature resplendent in pink and green plumage, that lived in remarkable amity with the galloping horses beside it. It was this beast which he had ridden last year, and his affection for it had remained constant.

Ruth hoisted him aloft and mounted the horse beside him. From her perch she looked down at the faces of those watching below, many of them known to her since childhood. The feel of the smooth wood between her knees, and the curly cold brass pillar between her hands, gave Ruth the same thrill that she remembered feeling years ago. Tonight, with her decision to stay at Thrush Green still fresh in her mind, the fact of being here on the day of the fair possessed an added poignancy.

For better or for worse, she was part and parcel of this

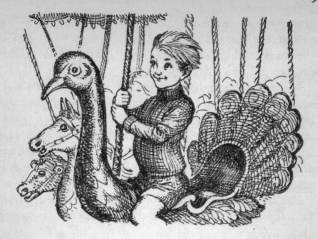

small world, and content to be so. Her spirits rose as the roundabout began to turn, and the music blared deafeningly from its centre. An archaic contraption, of organ-like appearance, emitted the noise, and Ruth watched Paul's admiring gaze fixed on the mirrors and jiggling marionettes which embellished the machine. She had wondered if violent motion would upset the child, but there was no sign of anything but holy ecstasy on her nephew's countenance.

The roundabout whirled faster and faster, and now the outside world was just a coloured blur, and Ruth and Paul had all they could do to stay on their flying mounts. As Paul soared up on his glorious ostrich, Ruth sank low upon her horse, and as the positions reversed Ruth caught glimpses of oily, creaking machinery, jerking and jumping, in the semi-darkness below the glittering organ. It looked remarkably rickety, and she turned her eyes hastily away.

One of the Curdles approached her, swaying easily among the heaving horses, and held out a black hand for the money. He shouted some pleasantry at Paul, but the noise was so deafening that the words were lost in the tumult. He flashed a smile at Ruth, dazzlingly white amidst the murk of his countenance, and continued his rolling progress.

At last the roundabout slowed down. The coloured blur, which had surrounded them, became individual figures; the houses, the church, the chestnut avenue, and the white palings of the village school ceased chasing each other and settled again into their appointed places, and Ruth and Paul descended, a trifle wobbly at the knees, but greatly exhilarated.

The ride had woken Paul from his earlier trance and now he dragged Ruth from one attraction to the next, chattering excitedly.

'Let's go on the switchback,' he cried. But Ruth felt that one dizzy ride was enough for a little while, and also, looking at the morose and battered Sam Curdle who was in charge, felt some repugnance.

'Look! Coconut shies!' carolled her nephew, tugging energetically at her arm. They hastened in the direction of the crowd which had collected there. Several youths, their shirt sleeves rolled up, hurled the small wooden balls savagely towards their target. The crack of wood against the wooden stands of securely placed coconuts alternated with the thwack of the balls against the taut canvas background. Very few coconuts fell off, despite the onslaught, but there were plenty of customers encouraged by Ben's lusty approval and Molly's pretty face.

'There's Molly!' shrieked Paul with joy, and, breaking from Ruth's grasp, fled across the battlefield in the thick of flying balls to join his friend.

'Oy!' shouted Ben, laughing. 'You'll get your 'ead knocked off for a coconut!' – which sally Paul thought the very essence of humour. He recognized Ben, despite a swelling cheek and some discoloration of the eye, as Molly's particular friend, and looked suddenly up at her with a questioning glance.

'He said he was coming to see you?'

'He did,' said Molly, nodding reassuringly at the little boy. He had known her feelings from the first and she did not intend to try and keep secrets from him now.

'Then it's all right?'

'It's all right,' repeated Molly, with such a delicious smile that Paul hugged her round the waist, in a sudden embrace that showed his joy, relief, and congratulations in one swift movement.

'Going to try your luck?' asked Ben, approaching.

'Please,' said Paul, and Ruth handed over sixpence. Ben gave Paul three balls and took him to the half-way line. While he took his stance solemnly and eyed the tempting coconuts, Molly inquired about the little boy's parents.

Ruth gave her news of their return in two days' time, and they exchanged gossip about their families. All the time, Ruth noticed, Molly's eyes followed the figure of the young man.

At last, as though wishing to share her pent-up happiness, Molly spoke rapidly to Ruth.

'I been to tea with Mrs Curdle today. That's her grandson, over there – Ben, his name. Paul knows about him, and p'raps you do too.'

'I don't, you know,' said Ruth, 'but he looks very handsome.'

Molly flushed with pride.

'He's a lot handsomer than that really, but he had a bit of a fight before tea.' Molly made it sound as though physical conflict before a meal was the most natural thing in the world, but she rattled on before Ruth could go further into this interesting disclosure.

'We've got to see my dad later, and I must say I don't relish it, but Ben don't show a bit of fear.'

'Does this mean you're thinking of leaving us?' asked Ruth tentatively.

'Not yet,' answered the girl, 'but I reckon I'll be gone before the winter.'

'Oh, Molly, we shall miss you!' said Ruth, putting out a hand with genuine concern. Molly smiled gaily at her.

'I'll be back next May the first,' she promised, 'with Curdle's Fair. Shall I look out for you, or will you be gone by then?'

Ruth shook her head slowly and returned Molly's smile.

'I'll be here,' she said.

At that moment Paul ran up, appealing for another sixpence.

'I hit one but it didn't fall off. Did you see? I hit one. Were you looking? I *actually* hit one! This time I'll knock it right off!'

'That's right,' said Ben. 'He'll get one this time, you see.'

Ruth handed over another sixpence and the two departed to try again. This time Paul's shots went wider than ever, but Ben spoke to Molly before returning to his customers and she vanished into a corner, returning with a coconut which she presented to the astounded Paul.

'But I didn't hit it!' he protested.

'Sh!' said Molly, one eye on the customers. 'It's what's called a consolation prize. You tried hard so Ben's give you this. Save a bit for me!' She gave the child a swift pat on the cheek, waved farewell, and returned to Ben's side.

Bearing the hairy trophy like some sacred relic, Paul, enraptured, led the way towards the swing-boats.

One of Mrs Curdle's daughters, as massive and dark, but

not a quarter as majestic as her mother, greeted them boisterously.

'Come along, my ducks. 'Op in now and give yerself a treat!' She lifted a long plank that was attached to the gear and applied it as a brake to the bottom of a scarlet boat. It slowed down abruptly, much to the vociferous annoyance of two young ladies who Ruth recognized as two of the genteel assistants at The Fuchsia Bush. Their refined accents had vanished under stress of circumstance and been replaced by a more plebeian, and far less painful, mode of speech.

They clambered out, displaying a prodigious amount of leg, and Paul began to climb the wobbly step-ladder that stood beside the swaying boat.

Ruth suddenly felt that she could not bear the motion of the swing so soon after the roundabout and the general noise which surrounded her.

'Can you work it alone? I'll wait here,' promised Ruth. Paul nodded his agreement, settled himself importantly on one red cushion, gripped the furry sally, still warm from the clutches of one of the young ladies, and began to haul himself into glorious motion.

'The young gentleman'll be all right, mum,' said Mrs Curdle's daughter heartily. 'If you gets nervous lift this 'ere stick, or 'oller for me. I'll be 'andy!' She bustled off to another client, leaving Ruth very content to stand alone enjoying the rush of air as Paul's boat beat its rhythmic way back and forth above her.

For Paul, had she known it, this solitary splendour was the highlight of his day. Always, for months and years now, he had longed to ride alone in a swing-boat, to be master of this flying craft, with no one to fuss about him or to slow his progress.

This, he told himself, as he soared blissfully above the trees on Thrush Green, this really was flying! He remembered his imaginary flight of the morning when he had peered inside the school, the church, and all the pleasant corners of Lulling. How much more satisfying was this heady swooping! He hauled vigorously, thrilled with his own prowess, and as the boat curved skywards he could see the pale lane that led to Nod and Nidden, and the buttercup fields that lay behind the little yard of the village school.

He must be nearly as high as the weathercock on the steeple, he told himself ecstatically. The light was beginning to thicken now, so that the sleepy grey town below the hill was indistinct, but in bright sunshine he was sure he could have seen every roof-top and chimney, and perhaps, still farther afield, the sea and glimpses of those foreign lands he so wanted to visit when he was a grown man.

He paused in his pulling for a moment, for his young arms were aching, and was content to swoop tranquilly back and forth while he mused upon those distant places that were beginning to welcome the sun which had now slipped away from Thrush Green. At this very minute, thought young Paul, there were people there laughing and playing – swinging perhaps, as he was, but on bright tropical trees that grew by seas as blue as the swing-boat that lay idle beside his own.

It was a game that he often played when he was alone, letting his mind dwell on things that were happening all over the world at the same moment, and today the motion of the swing-boat and the unaccustomed height added to the range of his fancies. A gleam of distant water caught his eye, and he knew that it was the River Pleshy where he picnicked and paddled on summer days. And now, as he swung on Thrush Green and over the sea those brown gay people played under their flowered trees, among the watery weeds of his much-loved river the minnows would be wavering in shoals, all headed up-stream, their eyes gleaming like jewels. And far away, in waters much more cold and turbulent, the great sharks would be splashing and diving. And farther still, sharks and a myriad other fishes, cruel or benign, slid mysteriously among the forests and caverns of the sea which helped to make this colourful round ball of a world the wonder that it was.

This power of transporting himself elsewhere was never to leave Paul. It came from a sympathy and kinship with all forms of life, and from an awareness of the smallness of the world around him. At the moment Thrush Green was his real world. He saw that the people there knew and relied on each other. It was a closely knit community of individuals, each sensitive to the other and related by ties of kinship, affection, dislike, or work. With the eyes of a six-year-old, Paul looked down upon the small familiar green face of his little world. In later years, after much travelling, he was to find the greater one about it very much the same.

Doctor Lovell had very few patients at his evening surgery, which did not surprise him. There is a therapeutic quality about a one-day fair that works more healing than a visit to the doctor.

Tomorrow, as he well knew, the sad familiar faces would line the walls of the waiting-room, but meanwhile, those that could forget their aches and pains had taken themselves and their children to enjoy the fun.

A message about Ella Bembridge's accident had been left on his desk and, now that the last patient had gone, he decided to walk along to the corner cottage.

The sky was a glory of colour, pink, gold, and mauve, with here and there a tinge of apple-green that told of the clear skies which had smiled all day upon the first of May.

Doctor Lovell stood by the gate enjoying the air and the

lively scene. At his side stood a young lilac tree, its buds now so tightly furled that they looked like bunches of red currants in the rosy light. Soon it would be adding its heady fragrance to the wallflowers and narcissi at his feet.

A man passed by with a bundle of stout bean poles balanced across his shoulder, and Doctor Lovell felt a pang of envy as he saw him, so confident that he would be here in Thrush Green to enjoy his beans in July and August, so secure in his plans and his provision for the future.

It was going to be hard to leave Thrush Green, if that were to be his fate. His eyes strayed to the Bassetts' house and his thoughts turned again to Ruth, as he had found them doing so often lately.

He opened the gate and turned left to pay his visit to Ella. The clamour of the fair blew like a blast from the green across the road, but above its noise a shrill voice could be heard.

'Look at me, doctor! Look at me!'

His first patient of the day attracted his attention. He waved cheerfully to the small flying figure, and would have passed on, but at the same instant he saw Ruth waiting patiently below.

With a heart behaving in a most unorthodox way for the property of a medical man, Doctor Lovell left the path of duty and joined the girl.

15. Mr Piggott Gives His Consent

DIMITY DEAN, a little weary in body, sat in the creaking wicker armchair in the corner of her patient's bedroom.

To the observer it would have appeared a serene domestic scene. Dimity was engaged in knitting a grey jumper, to enhance her mouse-like appearance the following winter, while Ella, propped against her pillows, perused the magazines which Mrs Bailey had left.

The reading-lamp beside the bed shed its light upon the fading narcissus flower still perched over one ear. The large cat had settled itself comfortably upon the bed, and soon the curtains would be drawn against the night which was beginning to envelop Thrush Green.

The noise of the fair was muted by the closed window, but the bright lights of the revolving roundabout and switchback passed and repassed across the low ceiling of the little room.

The scene may have looked peaceful but Ella's stringent comments on her reading matter contrasted strongly with her tranquil surroundings.

'Now, here's a damfool idea!' protested Ella energetically, folding back the thick magazine with a loud cracking noise. 'Sticking something you've broken together again, painting the cracks with scarlet lacquer, and giving it away to a friend! Wouldn't be a friend for long, I'd say! Can you beat it?'

She glowered upon the picture with some relish, before turning over.

'And this is even worse! Listen to this, Dim. "How to make a set of dainty table mats." And how I do hate "dainty"!' gibbered Ella, in a frenzied aside.

'How do you?' asked Dim equably, genuinely interested.

'I'll tell you,' said Ella, with fiendish satisfaction in her tone. 'You cut up pieces of lino that you have no further use for –'

'Like that bit in the shed,' exclaimed Dimity, eyes brightening.

'Like that bit in the shed,' conceded Ella grimly. 'That is if you *really want* dinner mats made of lino covered with mildew like prussian-blue fur, or even just made of lino *without* the prussian-blue fur —'

'Well, go on,' said Dimity.

'I *am* going on,' shouted Ella rudely, 'but you keep interrupting.'

'You'll upset the fireguard,' warned Dimity.

'Do you, or do you not, want to hear about these infernal mats?' inquired Ella furiously.

'Why, yes,' cried Dimity. Ella turned back to the magazine and continued truculently.

'Then you cut out sprays of flowers from plastic material. And then you stick these horrible sprays on to the lino mats, varnish the lot and there you are. As evil a set of vicious-looking table mats as ever saw the dim religious light of any church bazaar!'

She leant back upon her pillows contemplating these innocent suggestions as if they had been some dreadful rites connected with Black Magic. Dimity hastened to change the subject.

'I think it's time you had a dose of medicine for your rash.'

Ella continued to watch the lights revolving dizzily across the ceiling for a minute. When she spoke it was in a changed tone.

'D'you know, Dim, I feel quite extraordinary. Whether it's those dam' lights, or something I've eaten, I don't know, but I feel jolly queasy.'

Dimity, with a guilty start, recalled Dotty Harmer's quince jelly.

'Could be that ghastly fish in parsley sauce,' continued Ella speculatively. 'Never could stomach the stuff. Might as well eat whitewash or that muck they make you swallow before X-rays.'

She turned a searching glance upon the wilting Dimity.

'You feel all right? You ate it.'

'Well, yes,' faltered poor Dimity. 'I feel quite fit, but –' She hesitated, wringing sad limp hands still rosy from the dye.

'But what?' asked Ella. Her face was contorted with a sudden spasm of pain and she put a hand upon her capacious stomach.

Dimity took a brave deep breath and made her confession.

'I forgot to tell you – that quince jelly, dear. It was made by Dotty. She sent it up this afternoon.'

Groaning, Ella sank back upon the pillows.

'You're a fine friend!' she said roundly, but her gruff tone held a hint of kindliness. 'You know Dotty. She probably put a cupful of hemlock in to give it a bit of a kick!'

'Oh, Ella darling!' moaned poor Dimity, 'I wouldn't have had it happen for worlds. What shall we do?'

'Don't suppose it'll be fatal,' answered Ella morosely. 'Though with all I've got at the moment death would be a mercy, and that's flat! I'll get young Lovell to give me some jollop when he comes.'

She looked at her friend and gave her a sudden warm smile.

'Cheer up, Dim, it might be worse! Pull the curtains and shut out those vile lights. That'll help.'

Dimity crossed to the window and looked out upon the bustle and glitter of Mrs Curdle's fair across the road.

'Why,' she exclaimed, 'there is Doctor Lovell! And it looks like Ruth he's talking to! Yes, it is. I can see Paul running up to them.'

'Time that child was in bed,' snorted Ella. 'Ruth should know better, keeping him up while she philanders with her young man.'

'Oh, Ella, really!' protested Dimity.

'It's been sticking out a mile for weeks,' said Ella firmly,

her pains momentarily forgotten. 'If they don't make a
match of it before the year's out, I'll eat my hat. But not
tonight,' she added hastily, as Dotty's jelly made itself
felt.

'He's coming this way,' said the watcher at the window
suddenly. 'He must be calling here.'

'Then for pity's sake get him up here quickly,' urged her
friend. 'He'll find plenty to do.'

Sure enough, within two minutes the knocker was being
attacked and soon young Doctor Lovell confronted his
patient. Although he could not take to this brusque ungainly
woman, yet so warm and radiant is the power of love that
the doctor found himself feeling a new sympathy. The
unaccustomed sparkle in his dark eye and his gentle manner
only confirmed the suspicions of his tough spinster patient.
Here indeed was a man in love.

He examined the scalds and the rash and listened sympathetically to Dimity's incoherent confession. This was not
his first encounter with Dotty's handiwork. He smiled be-
nignly as he scribbled down a prescription on his little pad,
and took out two white pills from his case.

'These will help at the moment,' he promised Ella. 'Nurse
is coming with the cage for your legs and I really think
you'll feel much better tomorrow.'

'I should hope so,' responded the patient feelingly. 'What
a day! I never thought so much could happen to me in one
day.'

'Nor me,' agreed the young man warmly, but his tone held
a wonder lacking in his patient's. He stood for a moment as
though his thoughts were engaged elsewhere on Thrush
Green. The sardonic gaze from the bed brought him to his
senses.

'I'll see you in the morning,' he said hastily, collecting his belongings. 'You're a pretty straightforward case, you know. Burns, shock, dermatitis, and now this last disease.'

'D'you know what it is?' asked Ella.

'Unique to the district, ma'am, so I understand,' said young Doctor Lovell, smiling from the doorway. 'Dotty's Collywobbles!'

From among the noisy activity of the coconut shies Molly Piggott watched young Doctor Lovell emerge from Miss Bembridge's house and make his way briskly back to Doctor Bailey's.

'Wonder how he found the poor old dear?' thought Molly to herself, descending from the rapturous heights which she had inhabited for the last few hours for a brief visit to the everyday world of Thrush Green. But on such an evening the affairs of anyone as mundane as Ella Bembridge could hold Molly's attention but momentarily, for here, beside dear Ben, accepted by his grandmother, and with the future glittering as brightly as the fair itself, enchantment lay.

But despite her joy, one shadow remained. Her father had yet to be informed of her plans and Molly dreaded the encounter for Ben's sake. She had cast anxious eyes towards the cottage for the past two hours, but the windows had remained dark. The master of the house was still enjoying his leisure under the hospitable roof of The Two Pheasants next door.

At last Molly saw a light in the window and her heart sank. Now she was for it, she told herself. Best cut across home, fry the old boy's supper and rasher and egg, and break the news as best she could. She turned to Ben and put a hand upon his arm. The noise was deafening about them, and although the girl put her mouth within an inch of Ben's bruised ear, she could not make herself heard. Only by nodding in the direction of the cottage did she make her meaning clear.

Ben took her arm, calling as he did so to Rachel's father who was leaning dreamily against a booth negligently picking his teeth with the end of a feather.

'Take over, Bob, will you, for a bit?' shouted Ben. 'Be back in half an hour.'

Bob nodded casually, and strolled towards the coconut shies.

'Won't make a fortune there for the next half-hour, I'll lay,' said Ben grimly. 'But never mind, my gal, let's get over and see your dad.'

Molly stood still and looked at Ben with eyes dark with worry.

'Hadn't I best go back alone? I always gets his supper, see, my nights off, and I could easy tell him a bit about us, without your botherin'. He can be a bit nasty – short-like, you know, if he's surprised or anything. I don't want no unpleasantness, not on a lovely day like this has been.'

'This is my business, Moll, as well as yours and his. If there's any unpleasantness I'm the one to stop it. You needn't fear I won't behave civil in your father's house. My Gran's learnt me proper manners, you know, but this 'ere's a man's job. You cook his supper and I'll break the news while you breaks the eggs. How's that?'

He put his head on one side and gave her his crooked smile. Molly nodded silently, too moved with relief and love for speech.

Together they crossed the soft spring grass towards the cottage. The blare of the fair faded behind them and the rustle of the trees in the warm night air could be heard again.

'This is Ben, Dad. Ben Curdle – from the fair,' said Molly.

She was smiling bravely, but her heart fluttered in a cowardly way.

'Oh, it is, is it?' grunted her father. He had been rooting in the table drawer when they had entered and now faced them with a pointed knife in his hand and an expression of extreme disgust upon his sour old face.

' 'Evening, sir,' said Ben pleasantly. Mr Piggott turned his back and continued to rummage in the drawer.

'I'm trying to rustle up a bit of grub for meself,' grumbled the old man. 'Most nights I has to fend for meself, but Fridays I reckons to find a bit ready for me after a hard day's work.'

'I'll get you something,' broke in Molly swiftly. 'Bacon and egg I was going to do. You sit down and talk to Ben.'

'What for?' asked Mr Piggott looking at the young man with loathing. 'I never had no truck with gyppos all me life and I don't intend to start now. What you bring him in the house for, I'd like to know?'

Molly's blue eyes began to blaze.

'Ben here's a friend. And we don't want no talk about gyppos neither. Ben and me –'

'It's all right, Moll,' said Ben, with disarming gentleness. 'You go and see about the supper.'

'And who might you think you are?' shouted Mr Piggott with a belligerence born of six pints of beer on an empty stomach. 'Whose house is this? Yours or mine? You clear off over the green, where you come from. Sticking your nose into decent folks' houses and laying down the law –' He raised his right elbow threateningly, the dinner knife wavering dangerously near Ben's throat.

Ben grabbed the older man's wrist and lowered him forcibly into the wooden armchair that stood by the table. Mr Piggott sat down with a jerk and Ben quietly removed the knife from his grasp.

'God help us!' exploded Mr Piggott, attempting to bounce to his feet again. Ben's hand on his shoulder thwarted his efforts, and something about the glint in the young man's eye, despite his steady smile, seemed to flash a warning to Mr Piggott's beer-fuddled sense. He took refuge in pathetic bellowings to Molly in the kitchen.

'Here, Moll, what's all this about? Your poor old dad beaten up by this young gyppo – ted then, if you don't like gyppo,' he added hastily, as the grip on his shoulder tightened. 'Molly, who is this chap? You come on in here and see what he's a-doing!'

Molly put a mischievous face round the door and she and Ben exchanged a swift smile.

'I told you, Dad, it's Ben Curdle. You and him's going to have a little talk while I cooks your supper. Two rashers, Ben?' she asked.

'He's not having no rashers,' stormed her father. 'Not a morsel or bite of my hard-earned bread passes 'is lips –'

'Now, Dad,' remonstrated Molly, advancing further into the room. 'Ben's as hungry as you are. You'll talk better together over a meal.'

'If you take it easy, sir,' put in young Ben, 'maybe a drop of something from next door might help the meal along.'

Mr Piggott's black visage was softened into the near-semblance of a smile.

'Now that's talking sense, boy. Double X for me, unless you fancies something stronger yourself. Get the boy a jug, Moll, and get a move on, will you?'

He settled back in his chair and watched Ben vanish round the door. From the kitchen came the fragrance and sizzling of frying rashers and the sound of a daughter hard at woman's work.

Mr Piggott licked his wet lips and sat back well content.

By the time Ben returned Molly had set the cloth and was bearing in three plates. Mr Piggott had bestirred himself to the extent of lifting down from the dresser two thick glass mugs, souvenirs of the Coronation of Her Majesty Queen Elizabeth II, and placing them expectantly upon the table.

His eyes brightened as Ben deposited a foaming jug of draught beer by the cruet and he became even more jubilant when Ben pulled a half-bottle of whisky from his pocket and put it deferentially before him.

'Now that's very handsome of you, me boy,' said Mr Piggott, his voice husky with emotion. 'Very handsome indeed. Maybe you ain't so black-hearted as you looks.'

This, Molly knew, was as honeyed a speech as would ever fall from her parent's lips, and the only hint of apology that Ben could expect. They broached the meal with relish. Molly was surprised to find how hungry she was, and her father's unlovely open-mouthed mode of mastication for once failed to nauseate her.

Ben prudently waited until the plates were empty and his host's first mugful had been drained before approaching the business in hand. Then, characteristically, he came directly to the point.

'Molly and me's hoping to get wed some day, Mr Piggott.'

'Oh, ah!' said Mr Piggott carelessly, refilling his glass. He appeared oblivious of the importance of this remark, but fixed all his attention on the billowing head of froth that wavered at the brink of the mug.

Ben spoke a little louder.

'We've been friends like for a year now.' He looked across at Molly with a quick smile, and she nodded, smiling, in reply.

'That's right, Dad,' she said earnestly. A look of annoyance crossed her pretty face as she saw the complete absorption of her father in his brimming mug. Her voice became tart.

'You listening? Ben's trying to tell you something important. I shan't be here to cook your suppers much longer.'

This practical attack on his creature comforts had the desired effect. Mr Piggott raised his rheumy eyes and his habitual expression of truculence reappeared.

'What say? Not be here? What's all this?'

'I been saying,' Ben said patiently, 'as Molly and I wants to get married –'

'Too late!' asserted Mr Piggott, in his sexton's voice of authority. 'Dark now. Can't get married this time o' night. Besides I've swep' up the church.'

'We wasn't thinking of tonight, sir,' said Ben, trying to control the laughter in his voice. 'This summer, say – later on, before we lays up the fair for the winter.'

Mr Piggott, slightly glazed, looked a little more mollified.

'Can't stop you, I suppose. People gets married day in and day out – no reason why you and Molly shouldn't.'

His gaze wandered to the whisky bottle and his eyes widened pleasurably.

'What say we puts a dash o' this in along o' the beer?' he suggested enthusiastically to Ben. Molly shook her head violently at the young man.

'Oh, I wouldn't broach it now,' said Ben with studied carelessness. 'It's a little present for yourself. You open it sometime when I'm not here.'

Mr Piggott considered this suggestion earnestly, the mug at his lips and his eyes still caressing the whisky bottle.

'Ah, you got something there, boy,' he said at last, with the hint of a hiccup. 'I'll have more on me own. Have the lot, eh? Do me good, won't it?'

'Hope so,' said Ben briefly.

'Dad,' said Molly, leaning across the table and putting one

hand upon her father's. 'D'you know what we've said? We wants to get married and I hopes you'll say you're pleased.'

'Oh, I'm pleased all right – I'm pleased!' gabbled Mr Piggott in a perfunctory manner. 'You get married any time you like – summer or something you said, didn't you? Suits me. I'll get the church spruced up. Don't make no odds o me. All part of the day's work getting the place ready for weddings. Funerals too, come to think of it.' He turned a speculative eye upon the young pair.

'Wedding'd be more in your line, I reckons,' he conceded. 'If I was you I'd wait a bit for the funeral.'

With a sudden sigh he put his arms round his mug and the beloved whisky bottle, and, pillowing his head upon the empty greasy plate, fell instantly asleep.

Ten minutes later Molly and Ben, with the washing-up done and stacked away, stood at the open door.

Ben looked back at the snoring figure at the table.

'I suppose you might say we've got your father's consent,' he said to Molly.

And putting his arm round her waist he jumped her lightly from her doorstep and led her back to the joyful brightness of the fair.

16. Doctor Bailey Asks for Help

DOCTOR LOVELL returned from Ella's to Doctor Bailey's house.

His eyes wandered over the crowd that now thronged Curdle's fair, but Ruth and Paul were hidden somewhere among the mass.

It was a perfect evening, he told himself, and it had been a perfect day. The air was still warm, and scented with a myriad blossoms of spring; and in the bright light shed by the strong electric bulbs of the fairground the small young leaves fluttered like yellow mimosa against the dark-blue sky.

It was heady sort of weather, young Doctor Lovell thought. Heady enough to make anyone think of love. Half-defiant, half-amused, and wholly happy he surveyed his present plight and found it good.

He was hurrying back to see Doctor Bailey in response to a note left on the surgery desk. It had said :

Spare me a few minutes during the evening, will you? Any time after surgery to suit you.

$$D.B.$$

It was probably about a new case, thought the young doctor, or a message from the hospital delivered in his absence. He enjoyed these little encounters with the older man and never tired of hearing his salty and wise comments on the Lulling characters he was beginning to know almost as well as Doctor Bailey himself.

He walked into the hall, and tapped lightly on the sitting-room door.

He found Doctor Bailey sitting on the sofa, his thin legs covered with a dashing tartan rug and *The Times* crossword, almost completed, on his lap.

Mrs Bailey put aside her needlework and rose to greet him.

'Come and keep Donald company,' she said, indicating her chair.

'No, no,' protested the young man, 'I'll sit over here.'

'I'm just going to do some telephoning and sort out magazines for the hospital,' said Mrs Bailey. 'You couldn't have come at a better moment.'

She smiled conspiratorially at young Doctor Lovell as he held the door for her and went about her affairs.

'Come and get us both a drink,' said Doctor Bailey, removing his spectacles and flinging *The Times* to the floor.

The young man poured two glasses of sherry carefully at the tray standing ready on the side-table and brought them to the sofa.

'To Mrs Curdle and her fair!' said Doctor Bailey, nodding his head towards the window before sipping his wine.

'Mrs Curdle!' echoed young Doctor Lovell solemnly, sipping too. He put his glass carefully on the hearth and looked expectantly at the old man.

'How are you enjoying it all here?' asked Dr Bailey.

'Love it,' answered Doctor Lovell emphatically.

'That makes it easier for me then. I've at last made up my mind. It's taken me weeks of shilly-shallying, but now it's done I feel a good deal happier.'

He looked shrewdly across his glass to the young man.

'You know what I'm talking about?'

'I think so,' said Doctor Lovell soberly. His thin dark face was grave, for his heart was filled with pity and admiration for the older man. One day, he thought, I shall be facing this.

Doctor Bailey watched the young man closely and liked what he saw. There was no thought of self in that serious face, but an appreciation of a job to be bravely done. He spoke more freely.

'It's like this. I realize I shall never be able to do much again. If I can take four or five surgeries a week and attend a few of the real old folk who prefer to have me – well, that's about all I can hope to do. The point is – would you be willing to come in with me and bear the larger part of the practice on your shoulders?'

'There's nothing I'd like more, sir,' answered the young man earnestly. Doctor Bailey gave a gusty sigh of relief.

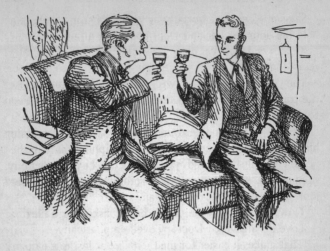

'Thank God for that! I'll tell you frankly, there's no one I'd like better to have with me and no one hereabouts better liked by the people. You'll fit in ideally.'

A thought seemed to strike him and he leant forward, peering intently at his companion.

'But look here, boy, I don't want you to make your mind up too hurriedly. Think it over. It's a big step to take, you know. Winnie always says: "Sleep on it," and she's usually right. Let me know in the morning.'

Doctor Lovell smiled for the first time in the interview. It was a slow warm smile that illuminated his long dark face and made it suddenly youthful.

'It's the finest offer I've ever had in my life. I was beginning to wonder if I could ever bear to leave Lulling – and now, this! It's perfect.'

Doctor Bailey raised his glass.

'To our practice, then.' They drank together, and Doctor Bailey replaced his glass with fresh energy.

'Now, the position is this. This particular practice is

really just about big enough for a man and half. That's fine at the moment. You have to be the man, and probably a bit more, and I'm your half a man.' He smiled wryly, but cheerfully.

'As you know, the other four chaps in partnership in the town cover most of the southern area, but although our district is sparsely populated I believe you'll find that you'll have enough for two men here in time. There's a new estate going up at Nidden and a batch of council houses along the main road to the north. So that if you decide to settle here you should find a growing practice and could take a partner in with you.'

'That's a long way ahead, I hope,' said young Doctor Lovell.

'I shan't last for ever,' said old Doctor Bailey, 'but I know this. I'll last a dam' sight longer with you to carry most of the load for me.'

'Then we're both satisfied,' said the young man. And sitting back he basked in the glow born of his good wine and his good fortune.

Twenty minutes later, having bidden the older man good night, young Doctor Lovell sat alone in the surgery. He had called in to collect some papers, but enjoyed the opportunity of complete privacy to savour to the full the wonderful news which he had just received.

Earlier in the day he had realized how much Thrush Green and his work there had really meant to him. Now, in a few minutes, he had been offered his life's happiness – work which he knew he could do well, in a place and among people dear to him.

Outside the fair throbbed and spun merrily, and its cheerful raucous music found an echo in the singing in his own heart. May the first – a day of enchantment. He would never forget it, he told himself! He remembered the doctor's first toast to Mrs Curdle and her fair. Long may she reign, thought happy young Doctor Lovell, and bring as much joy each first of May as she had done today!

He took a cigarette from his case and was surprised to see that his fingers shook. He crossed to the window and looked out upon the gay scene spread beneath the dark curve of the night sky.

Over in the Bassetts' house an upstairs light was burning. It was the landing light, young Doctor Lovell observed, which meant that his first patient of the day was now safely in bed after all his excitements, and his aunt would be free downstairs.

Suddenly young Doctor Lovell felt that he must tell someone of the good news which fermented and bubbled within him. He had meant to follow Mrs Bailey's habitual advice and 'sleep on' his secret before he made it known, but now, young, lonely, and bursting with excitement, he knew that he must go to Ruth and let her share his happiness.

Who knows, thought the young man as he crossed the grass with the clamour of the fair ringing in his ears, this very day may prove to be the start of a new life for us both at Thrush Green?

The gate clanged noisily behind him, and for a moment he leant with his back against it, watching the lighted hall through the glass door, suddenly half-fearful of approaching the girl.

As he stood there, his heart throbbing as madly as the fair behind him, Ruth opened the door with a wide welcoming gesture.

'How lovely to see you,' she cried. 'Come in, come in!'

And Doctor Lovell knew that his happiness was complete.

Upstairs Paul had been in bed for an hour, but found it impossible to sleep. So much had happened in the day. He had been pronounced cured of his illness, which meant that he could go back to school on Monday, and would be free to play all day tomorrow, which was Saturday, and to watch the departure of Mrs Curdle's fair if he were awake in time.

He had seen Molly united with her Ben and knew that her worries were ended. But, best of all, his sleepy memories were those of the glittering, noisy, spinning fairground, home of that near-deity Mrs Curdle, and Ben, who now shone as a hero in Paul's eyes, for he had overheard two gossipers discussing the fight and had noticed the scars borne by both men.

Tomorrow, or Sunday, he knew that his father and mother would be home again and his heart leapt at the thought. He turned over and felt the cool pillow against his flushed cheek. Across the mirror on his wardrobe the lights of the fair twinkled, signalling across the darkness their message of gaiety and shared excitement, both tonight and in the future.

From the landing came an equally comforting light through the half-open door. If the flickering lights in the mirror spoke of dizzy excitement the one from the landing spoke of loving care and security. Between the two Paul felt himself swinging gently towards sleep, the lilt of the music from the fair in his ears and the motion of the swing-boat, rocking beneath the stars, still stirring in his veins.

The clanging of the gate caught him back to consciousness again, and he heard Aunt Ruth open the front door.

'Come in, come in!' he heard her cry, so happily, so warmly, that he knew his young aunt's troubles had vanished as swiftly and suddenly as Molly's had done.

Everything would be right now, Paul thought dreamily,

eyelids drooping again, and his last clear thought was – what more would you expect of May the first? Everything was bound to turn out right on such a magical day.

Within two minutes he was asleep, and for him the splendid day was ended.

17. Doctor Bailey Gives Help

THROUGH the little window of her caravan Mrs Curdle saw the light in the surgery suddenly vanish, and, a minute later, she observed Doctor Lovell's tall figure crossing the grass towards the Bassetts' house. She took a deep breath, and tried to calm the fluttering of her heart. She must muster all the courage she could and make the dreaded visit, which the young doctor's comings and goings during the past hour or so had delayed for her.

Not that Mrs Curdle had been idle while she had waited with one eye cocked on the tall grey house of her old friends. When she had returned from her routine inspection of the fair she had settled herself on the red plush stool which stood by the stove and had set about her usual Friday-evening business of putting out the wages for her workers. This she would do, she told herself, before making herself clean and tidy for her annual visit to the doctor. Who knows what shape she might be in on her return? What news of fearful illness she might bear back with her? More frightening still, supposing that the doctor took her straight to that dreaded hospital of terrible memories?

Mrs Curdle, old and in pain, felt her fears thronging round her like a flock of dark evil bats, mis-shapen, mocking – the arbiters of doom. But, old and frail as she was, her grim courage remained, a tiny impregnable fortress standing sturdily against the onslaughts of a myriad doubts and fears. She thrust them resolutely away from her, and fetching the old card table which had once held her crystal, she set it up as she had done every Friday night for over thirty years.

She pulled out the battered case, which had caused so much trouble that afternoon, and began to count out notes, silver, and coppers, licking a dusky thumb every now and again, and saying the amounts to herself aloud.

Mrs Curdle needed no list to help her in her task. She had no account book, no notes, no jottings, to confuse or help her calculations. Beneath the coils of black hair Mrs Curdle's shrewd mind knew to a penny just what was due to each man, woman, and child under her management. The piles were stacked methodically in lines on the table, little heaps weighted with neatly piled silver and copper, with Sam Curdle's final earnings in their accustomed place in the row.

Mrs Curdle put the malefactor's dues ready with neither resentment nor pleasure. All her life she had, of necessity, been decisive and forward-looking. There had never been time in her busy life, nor had she ever had the inclination, to look back unnecessarily. What was done, was done; and remorse and regrets had never played much part in the old lady's life. Sam had failed her. He must go. It was as simple as that.

From time to time she looked across at Doctor Bailey's house. She had seen his young helper go in and later had caught a glimpse of him through the surgery window. With half her mind she welcomed his presence there for it postponed her own going.

She put out the large brass bowl on the minute dresser. It stood, twinkling and flashing, as it caught the light from the hanging oil-lamp above the table, awaiting the rustle and clatter of that evening's takings when the Curdles arrived later to tip in their contributions and collect their wages. Then she covered the laden table with a multi-coloured shawl of vivid brightness to keep the money safe from prying eyes and any draughts which might remove a stray note. Mrs Curdle's business arrangements were completed once again and she turned to her personal preparations.

The surgery light still shone as Mrs Curdle washed her massive arms and shoulders at the diminutive basin near the stove. She washed her face and neck and gazed at her reflection sadly as she dabbed herself dry with a small striped towel.

The little mirror, at which her husband had shaved so many years before, gave Mrs Curdle a dim and distorted copy of her features, but she was comforted to see that she had some colour in her cheeks, and that though black shadows lay like sooty smudges beneath her eyes, the eyes themselves were as bright as ever.

Her gold ear-rings looked as fine as the day on which her bridegroom had given them to her, and after combing and replaiting her hair, Mrs Curdle donned her best black satin frock, a new black cardigan, and her largest checked shawl, and looked again from her window.

The light vanished and Mrs Curdle's throat constricted with sudden fear. Almost at once she saw young Doctor Lovell hasten down the path and emerge upon Thrush Green.

Mrs Curdle took a last look at her caravan. All lay in readiness for her return, all was in order. The diminutive stove seemed to wink encouragement, the lamp swung as though nodding a kindly farewell, and all the small dear objects which had shared her tiny home and her long life seemed to return to their troubled mistress some of that love which she had given them.

With the bunch of flowers – the largest and most beautiful she had ever made – in one hand, and the ebony stick in the other, Mrs Curdle descended the steps of her home, and with slow dignity approached the house of Doctor Bailey.

Mrs Bailey came from the little back room, where she had been packing up the magazines, to answer the door. Mrs Curdle, tall and imposing in her best black, stood on the doorstep with the bright lights of her fair behind her and the great bouquet before her.

'With my compliments, ma'am, as always,' she said, graciously inclining her head, and handing in the dazzling blooms.

'They are more magnificent every year,' said Mrs Bailey truthfully, ushering in her guest. She looked with genuine admiration at the great mop-heads fashioned with such skill and patience. Scarlet, orange, pink, and mauve, they flaunted their gaudy beauty like some tropical exotic blooms compared with the modest narcissi that sent their gentle perfume from the hall table.

'Come and see how well last year's bunch has worn,' said Mrs Bailey. 'The doctor's looking forward to seeing you.'

She led the way into the sitting-room and Mrs Curdle followed, her dark eyes glancing round the hall as she went. Houses made Mrs Curdle ill at ease. There was so much space, so many bare places on the walls, so far to walk. It seemed to the old lady that there was nothing home-like about such a place. Her own caravan, with everything within arm's reach, fitted her as snugly as a snail's shell. The sight of so much floor to sweep and walls to clean appalled her, and the lofty ceilings made her feel lost and unsafe.

'Might as well live in a church,' thought Mrs Curdle to herself, as she picked her way gingerly over the unaccustomed carpet. ' 'Twould never do for me.'

The doctor came forward to greet her, both hands outstretched and a welcoming smile on his lined old face.

'Come and sit down, Mrs Curdle. We've been looking forward to seeing you all day. It wouldn't be May the first, you know, without a visit from you.'

He drew forward a straight-backed armchair, and Mrs Curdle seated herself regally. Mrs Bailey brought forward last year's bouquet for the old lady's inspection.

'It do seem to have kep' very nice,' agreed Mrs Curdle, with satisfaction. 'It pays to use a good dye, I always say. And you takes good care of them, I can see that,' she added politely.

They talked of many things, the fortunes of the fair, the news of Lulling and Thrush Green friends, the death of one of the nurses who had attended her so long ago at Lulling Hospital, the floods which the overflowing River Pleshy had caused earlier in the year, and other general matters.

'I hope that you are not thinking of giving up,' said the doctor. 'We've heard all sorts of rumours, you know.'

Mrs Curdle's face grew grave.

'There's times I think I must,' she said slowly. 'I been none too good lately. I was going to have a word with you about it all.'

Mrs Bailey rose quietly.

'I'll leave you to talk, and I'll go and cut some sandwiches.'

Mrs Curdle looked alarmed.

'None for me, ma'am, thanking you kindly. My stomach's been that queasy, I can't tell you, and I'll have a sup of something later on before I gets to bed.'

'That doesn't sound too good,' said Doctor Bailey, as his wife retreated to her magazine-packing, closing the door firmly upon the tête-à-tête which she knew to be so important.

He hitched his chair nearer to Mrs Curdle's and looked closely at her.

'Let's see your tongue,' he said suddenly. Mrs Curdle put it out obediently.

'Horrible!' said the doctor with professional relish. 'Tell me all about this trouble and then I'll have a real look at you.'

Mrs Curdle gave a sigh, half of bewilderment and half of relief. Now that she was actually under the doctor's roof, with his reassuring presence so close at hand, her fears seemed suddenly less potent. She began to talk falteringly.

'It's been comin' on a long time now – best part of five years, I'd say. Catches me, sir, back and front.' She gripped the small of her back bending forward and fixing anguished dark eyes upon the doctor. He nodded sympathetically.

'Makes me dizzy,' went on Mrs Curdle, warming to her theme. The relief of pouring out her long-pent-up troubles gave her an unaccustomed eloquence.

'I has to sit down, my head gets that giddy. And today I had it that bad I fell right over – fainting, you might say. It's the pain, Doctor, a burning kind of pain, that flares up in me middle.'

She knotted a gnarled fist and pressed it fiercely against the jet buttons of her cardigan.

'And can you eat?' asked Doctor Bailey, remembering her prodigious appetite in earlier times.

'Scarce a morsel,' asserted Mrs Curdle, with mournful pride. 'I takes no breakfast these days, though I cooks for young Ben regular. Just a drop of tea, and maybe a bit of bread if the pain ain't too nigglin'.'

'What time did you faint today?' inquired the doctor. Mrs Curdle wrinkled her brow with concentration.

' 'Twould have been after dinner some time. I was taking a look round the show, I knows that.'

'Ah!' said Doctor Bailey. 'After your dinner, eh? And what did you have?'

'Pork chop and fried onions,' said the old lady. 'With a bit of good strong cheese to follow. Nothing rich or heavy like.'

The doctor looked with an experienced eye at his patient's drawn face and the hint of yellow about the eyes that told of biliousness. He could guess the sort of diet that Mrs Curdle's ancient stomach was called upon to digest day after day. The old lady had always been a great frying-pan cook, as of necessity were most of the tribe, and her tea, as the doctor remembered with an inward shudder, was of a strong Indian variety which was reckoned to be at its best after half an hour's stewing on the little hob. It was small wonder that her overtaxed digestive system had begun to rebel after more than seventy years of such treatment.

But there might be more to it than faulty diet, thought the old doctor, gazing speculatively at the earnest face before him. Mrs Curdle had lost her sparkle. There were mental as well as physical troubles to be blamed for that pinched unhappy look about her mouth and eyes. The doctor determined to know all, and set about it with his customary guile and kindly delicacy.

'I think we'll have to give you a little help over your diet, my dear. I'm positive that that's all that's wrong and you've nothing to worry about at all. Less fat, very little tea – and that weak – less bread and fried foods, and you'll be fighting fit in no time.'

Mrs Curdle bridled slightly.

'I eats next to nothing –' she began, in a hurt tone.

Doctor Bailey leant forward and patted her knee.

'I know you do, I know you do. But it's probably the wrong sort of food for you now. I'll write it down for you and you need not worry any more about it.'

Mrs Curdle looked mollified, and the doctor continued gently.

'You see, we're both getting older, Mrs Curdle, and our poor old bodies can't cope with the food – nor life itself – quite as bravely as they did when we first met. Why, for the last few weeks I've practically lived on milk.'

'You looks peaky,' agreed Mrs Curdle sagely. 'Maybe it's good food you needs.'

The doctor began to feel that he was making little headway, but he brushed aside her comment, and approached nearer to his objective.

'And because our bodies are old and tired, we begin to worry about them and that makes them worse. So it goes on. And when any little troubles arise – money matters, say, or quarrels in the family – they all seem so much worse than they really are.'

He noticed that a gleam had kindled in Mrs Curdle's eye, and she nodded her dark head in agreement.

'That's very true, sir. I've been that way myself this year with our Ben – dear George's boy, you remember?' The doctor nodded, fearful of speaking and breaking the flow of words which would help his old friend far more than any of his bottled medicine could.

'He's fair broke my heart, these last few months,' confessed the old lady. She settled her great bulk more comfortably against the back of the chair and told her sympathetic friend of all that she had endured. She told of Ben's moodiness, his sullen silences, his inexplicable neglect of the job which he had always taken such delight in, and the barrier which had grown up between them.

Out it all poured, the doctor listening intently to this simple but poignant tale. She told of her increasing depression, the more frequent attacks of pain, the silence which she kept, imposed upon her by her innate pride of spirit, which only aggravated the misery of both body and mind. She told of all her hopes of making young Ben a partner in the business which was the very essence of her being, and how those hopes had dwindled as the sad frustrating weeks had gone by.

Through it all, the doctor noticed, ran the strong double thread of her great love for Ben and the fair. They were both of her creating. They were as much part of her as the dusky right hand which smoothed the black satin to and fro, to and fro, over her massive knee as she spoke. If she lost either her life would be lopped of its vital force and purpose, and she would surely dwindle and die.

For want of breath Mrs Curdle paused, and the doctor gave what advice he could.

'I'm afraid it's all part of getting old, Mrs Curdle, this anxiety about keeping our affairs going well and wondering if the young ones will ever keep the boat afloat as well as we did. It's a right feeling, I suppose, but it does mean that we have to decide what is the right thing to do and the right time to do it. I've been having the same thing to face here.'

'You have?' said Mrs Curdle in surprise, projected momentarily from her inward-looking at her own troubles to those of her fellow, which was precisely what the wise doctor had wanted.

'You see,' said Doctor Bailey, smiling, 'I'm old too – older than you are, my dear – and very much more tattered and torn I'm afraid. I've been clinging to the hope that this illness would pass and that I would be quite able to continue as I always have done with my doctoring, but nature has said "No". It's been saying "No" for a long time,' admitted the doctor ruefully, 'but I've been too pig-headed to listen. But today I did listen, and I've made my decision.'

'And what's it to be?' asked Mrs Curdle.

'It's to be sensible. To face the fact that I'm growing old, that I must have help if I'm to be of any use to my patients. And another thing I've found out today. I am not indispensable. My young partner can do the job as well, and perhaps better, than I ever could do it.'

There was a sadness in her old friend's face that moved Mrs Curdle strangely although she had not fully understood all that the doctor had told her.

'You been the best doctor in the world,' she said stoutly. 'I never knew a better doctor – never!'

Doctor Bailey, knowing that he was the only one that had ever attended her, could not help being secretly amused, as well as touched, by her faith in him.

'Don't think I'm unhappy about it,' said the doctor truthfully. 'I'm glad. The work goes on, that's the comfort. I only wish I'd realized that years ago and saved myself a mint of heart-searching.'

He turned to the old lady.

'And that's what I want you to face, as I did. You must have help. Let someone share the load and you'll be of some use. Be too proud to ask for it and you'll go down under it. We're both in the same boat, my old friend.'

Mrs Curdle nodded thoughtfully. The doctor, seeing her engrossed in thought, imagined that she was trying to choose, from among her tribe, one best suited to her purpose.

'If Ben doesn't seem the man for it –' he began. But the old lady cut him short.

Eyes flashing, and back as straight as a ram-rod, Mrs Curdle answered indignantly :

'Who said Ben wasn't the man for it? There's nothing wrong with my Ben now. You never let me finish the tale!'

Humbly and hastily Doctor Bailey begged Mrs Curdle's pardon, secretly delighted at this flash of her old spirit.

And within five minutes he had heard of Ben's trans-

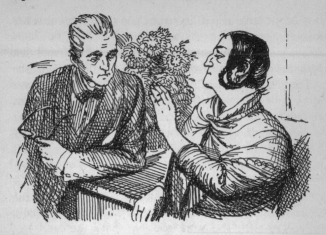

figuration, of his proposed marriage with young Molly
Piggott, and, best of all, of Mrs Curdle's decision to take him
into partnership that very day on her return to the caravan.

'We shan't forget this May the first, either of us, Mrs
Curdle,' said the doctor, when he had heard her out. 'You'll
see. My practice will go on, and your fair will go on.'

'They'll both go on!' agreed Mrs Curdle, with great
satisfaction.

The two old friends looked at each other and smiled their
congratulations.

'And now,' said Doctor Bailey briskly, 'I'm going to have
a look at you.'

Later, Mrs Curdle, with a light heart, crossed the road
again. She had made her parting from the Baileys in the
hall, but now with her feet on the grass of Thrush Green
she turned to look once more at the house where she had
received such comfort of body and mind.

Silhouetted against the light of the open doorway stood
the doctor and his wife, their hands still upraised in fare-

well. Mrs Curdle waved in return and turned towards her home.

In her cardigan pocket lay some pills and a simple diet sheet, but it was not of these that Mrs Curdle thought. She was thinking of Doctor Bailey whose good advice had never failed her throughout her long life. Her way now was clear.

With a tread as light as a young girl's, Mrs Curdle, her fears behind her, hurried to find Ben.

He should hear, without any more waste of time, of his good fortune and the future of the fair.

Meanwhile, the doctor and his wife had returned to the sitting-room. Mrs Bailey had carried in a tray with soup, fruit, and a milky drink, for, with their visitors, supper had been delayed and the hands of the silver clock on the mantelpiece stood at a quarter to ten.

They supped in silence for a while. Then Mrs Bailey, putting her bowl down, said:

'And does the fair go on?'

'Yes,' said the doctor. 'I'm thankful to say it does.'

The music surged suddenly against the window with renewed vigour, and they smiled at each other.

As Mrs Bailey stacked the tray she noticed that the doctor's eyes strayed many times to the gaudy bouquet which flamed and flared like some gay bonfire.

'I'll take those flowers to the larder shelf,' said Mrs Bailey, advancing upon them.

'No,' said her husband, and something in his voice made her turn and look at him. He sat very still and his face was grave. 'I'd like them left out.'

Mrs Bailey could say nothing.

'We shan't see the old lady again,' said Doctor Bailey. 'I doubt if she has three months to live.'

18. The Day Ends

AT half past ten the lights of Mrs Curdle's fair went out and the music died away. The last few customers straggled homewards, tired and content with their excitement, and by the time St Andrew's clock struck eleven Thrush Green had resumed its usual quietness.

A few lights, mainly upstairs ones, still shone from some of the houses around the green, but most of the inhabitants had already retired, and dark windows and empty milk bottles standing on the doorsteps showed that their owners were unconscious of the happenings around them.

The church, The Two Pheasants, and the village school were three dark masses, but a small light twinkled between the two latter. It shone from Molly Piggott's bedroom where the girl was undressing.

The blue cornflower brooch lay on the mantelshelf and beside it a small ring.

'You shall have a proper one, some day,' Ben had promised, 'not just a cheap ol' bit of trash from the fair.' But to Molly it was already precious – a souvenir of the most wonderful day in her life.

She had parted from Ben only a few minutes before, when he had told her of his new status in the business, and she had promised to be up early in the morning to see him again before the caravans set off on their journey northwards.

She clambered into the little bed, which lay under the steep angle of the sloping roof, keeping her head low for fear of knocking it on the beam above.

Carefully she set her battered alarm clock to five o'clock, wound it up, and put it on the chair close beside her. Then, punching a hollow in her pillow, she thrust her dizzy dark head into it and was asleep in two minutes.

In the next bedroom Mr Piggott, asleep in his unlovely underclothes as was his custom, stirred at the thumpings made by his daughter's bed and became muzzily aware of her presence in the house.

Vague memories of a young man, a bottle of whisky, and Molly's future swam through his mind. No one to cook for him, eh? No one to clear up the house?

'Daughters!' thought Mr Piggott in disgust. 'Great galli-vanting lumps, with no idea of doing their duty by their poor old parents!'

He relapsed into befuddled slumber.

Ruth Bassett's light still shone above the bed. She sat propped against the pillows, a book before her, but her attention was elsewhere.

Doctor Lovell had left an hour or so before and the mem-ory of their pleasant time together warmed her unaccount-ably. She had scrambled eggs in the kitchen while he had supervised the toast, and together they had sat at the kitchen table enjoying the result, brewing coffee, and talking incessantly.

She had never felt so at ease in anyone's company and the thought that he had sought her out to tell her his wonderful news touched her deeply. Plainly, he was as devoted to Thrush Green as she was. And who can blame him? thought Ruth, as a distant cry from one of the Curdle tribe reached her ears.

It had cured her of her misery and given her new hope. It had, as it had always done, provided her with comfort and contentment. Her decision to make her home there filled her with exhilaration. Tomorrow, when Joan and her husband returned, they would make rosy plans.

For a moment her mind flitted back to the cause of this decision. The figure of Stephen, tall and fair-haired, flickered in her mind's eye, but, try as she would, she could not recall his face. It seemed a shocking thing that one who had meant so much could so swiftly become insubstantial. The ghost of Stephen had vanished as completely as the man himself and, Ruth observed with wonder, her only feeling was of relief.

She put her book to one side, switched off the light and settled to sleep, secure in the knowledge that the dawn would bring no torturing memories, but only the wholesome shining face of Thrush Green with all it had to offer.

Young Doctor Lovell was writing a letter to his father, telling him of Doctor Bailey's offer, asking his advice about the financial side, and explaining the future possibilities of the practice.

He wrote swiftly in his neat precise handwriting and covered two pages before he paused. Then he lit a cigarette and stared thoughtfully at his landlady's formidable ornaments on the mantelpiece.

It is not in the nature of young men to open their hearts to their fathers and to tell them of their private hopes and feelings, particularly when a young woman is involved, and Doctor Lovell was no exception. But he was fond of his father – his mother had been dead for ten years – and he wanted him to know that this offer meant more to him than just a livelihood.

His thoughts turned again to Ruth. He knew now, without any doubt, that she would always be the dearest person in the world to him. As soon as she had recovered sufficiently from her tragedy to face decisions again he would ask her to marry him.

Life at Thrush Green with Ruth! thought young Doctor Lovell, his spirits surging. What could anyone want better than that?

Smiling, he picked up his pen and added the last line to his letter:

I know I shall always be very happy here.

He sealed it, propped it on the mantelpiece against a china boot, and went whistling to bed.

In her cottage nearby lay Miss Fogerty from the village school. She was fast asleep. Her small pink mouth was slightly ajar, and her pointed nose twitched gently over the edge of the counterpane, for all the world like some small exhausted mouse.

It had been a tiring day. The children were always so excited on fair day, and Friday afternoon meant that she had to battle with her register amidst the confusion of twenty or so young children playing noisily with toys brought from home – a special Friday-afternoon treat.

Her last thought had been a happy one. Tomorrow it was Saturday. If it were as lovely and sunny as today had been her weekly wash-day would be most successful, she told herself.

Her Clarks' sandals were prudently put out underneath the chair which supported her neat pile of small-clothes. Miss Fogerty was a methodical woman.

'No need to set the alarm,' she had said happily to herself as she folded back the eiderdown. 'Saturday tomorrow!'

And with that joyous thought she had fallen instantly asleep.

Ella Bembridge and Dimity Dean had taken the advice of Doctor Bailey and settled to sleep early.

Dimity had fallen into a restless slumber disturbed by confused dreams. She seemed to be standing knee-deep in a warm crimson pond, stirring an enormous saucepan full of parsley sauce, while Mrs Curdle and Ella stood by her, wagging admonitory fingers, and saying, in a horrible sing-song chant: 'Never touch the stuff – it's poison! Never touch the stuff – it's poison!'

Ella found sleeping impossible. Her legs hurt, her rash itched, and the shooting pains in her stomach, though somewhat eased by Doctor Lovell's white pills, still caused her discomfort.

Morosely, she catalogued the day's tribulations, as others, less gloomily disposed, might count their blessings.

'Visit to the doctor – a fine start to a day. Blasted parsley sauce. Rubber gloves. That boiling dam' dye. Dotty's colly-wobbles. Two more visits from doctors, to top the lot – and Mrs Curdle's hurdy-gurdy for background music! What a day!'

She glowered malevolently at Mrs Bailey's daffodils, a pale luminous patch in the darkness. One ray of hope lit her gloom.

'At least May the second shouldn't be quite as bad as May the first has been!'

Somewhat comforted, Ella moved her bulk gingerly in the bed, for fear of capsizing the leg guard, and waited grimly for what the morrow might bring forth.

Away in the fields below Lulling Woods the creator of poor Ella's latest malady lay in her bed.

Dotty Harmer's room was in darkness, lit only by the faint light of the starlit May sky beyond the grubby latticed panes.

Dimly discernible by Dotty's bed was a basket containing the mother cat and one black kitten. Much travail during the golden afternoon had only brought forth one pathetic little still-born tabby, sadly mis-shapen, and ten minutes later this fine large sister kitten. Dotty had buried the poor dead morsel in the warm earth, shaking her grizzled head and letting a tear or two roll unashamedly down her weatherbeaten cheeks.

The survivor was going to be a rare beauty. Dotty could hear the comfortable sound of a rasping tongue caressing the baby between maternal purrs, and cudgelled her brains for a suitable name.

'Nigger, Blackie, Jet, Night, Sooty – too ordinary!' decided Dotty, tossing in her bed.

She thought of the glorious day that had just passed and remembered the spring scents of her garden as she had awaited the birth.

'Should be something to do with May,' pondered Dotty. ' "May" itself would have done if it had been a pale kitten, but somehow – a dark little thing like that –' She resumed her meditations and the memory of Molly and her dark young man came floating back to her.

'Gipsy!' thought Dotty, groping towards the perfect name. She felt herself getting nearer. Something that was dark, magnificent, and connected with May the first, she told herself. It came in a flash of inspiration.

'Mrs Curdle!' cried Dotty in triumph.

And with the rare sigh of a satisfied artist, she fell asleep.

Gradually the lights dimmed in the old stone houses round Thrush Green, but still one shone in Doctor Bailey's house.

The good doctor himself was asleep. He had had the busiest day of his convalescence and had retired more exhausted than he would admit to his wife.

The last sad interview with Mrs Curdle had been a great

strain – greater because his grief had to be kept hidden behind his kindly professional mask in front of the old lady. Her case, he knew, was hopeless, and when her fair came to rest for the winter that year he had no doubt that she who had ruled its kingdom for so many years would be at rest too.

It gave the old doctor some consolation to know that he had helped her to assure the future of her little world, and that when next May Day came the full-blooded music of Mrs Curdle's fair would still shake the young leaves on Thrush Green and all its innocent pleasures would be there again in the capable young hands of Ben Curdle.

The thought that his own affairs too were as squarely arranged as Mrs Curdle's own gave him a deep inner peace. He had woken that morning with a battle to fight, and now that battle was over. Whether he had won or lost, the doctor was not sure, but now that the heat of it was over he could retire from the field with his duty well done.

The good old man slept easily.

But his wife could not sleep.

Her mind turned over the happenings of that sunlit day and refused to rest. She remembered the glory of her dewy garden, the coffee party with those dear odd creatures, the wonderful change in poor little Ruth, Ella's mishap, which had been a real blessing for it had forced her husband to make his decision, and – last of all, to her the most poignant happening of that long crowded day – her husband's disclosure of Mrs Curdle's doom.

She heard St Andrew's clock chime the quarter after eleven o'clock. Would she never sleep? Carefully, she crept from the great double bed and made her way to the kitchen to warm herself some milk. Sometimes this calmed her active mind and she hoped that the old-fashioned remedy would work now.

She carried her steaming mug to the sitting-room, switched on the small reading-lamp and sipped slowly.

The three or four street lamps round Thrush Green had gone out at eleven o'clock, for country dwellers are early abed. Through the window she could see the dark shapes of the caravans against the starlit sky. One or two still showed lights, for the Curdles had been busy since closing time collecting their weekly wages and putting their personal belongings together ready for an early start on the morrow.

Mrs Bailey looked with affection, and with infinite sorrow, at the ancient caravan which housed her good friend. Its old beautiful lines showed plainly against the clear night sky and its small window glowed from the lamp within. The light quivered and blurred before Mrs Bailey's tear-filled eyes, and she turned hastily away.

There was nothing to weep about, she told herself with as much firmness as she could muster. Mrs Curdle's long life neared its end, but her work would thrive and her family too. She would never be forgotten while they endured.

The peace of the sitting-room and the comforting warmth of the milk began to soothe Mrs Bailey. She looked at the loved things around her and suddenly realized what riches were gathered there together in one lovely drop of time.

There on the side-table stood the blue-and-white bowl, a wedding present from a long-dead friend, filled with narcissi which had forced their fragile beauty from the dark prison-house of earth so recently to delight her. An orange, which had travelled the far seas, touched its reflection in the black polished beauty of the Chinese chest on which it stood. The chest had been brought back in a tea-clipper by a sailor great-uncle of Mrs Bailey's, and its perfection had always stirred her. The mug from which she sipped had been a christening present to her son. That son, she remembered, who was much the same age of Mrs Curdle's dear George would have been.

She took a deep breath and looked with new eyes at her familiar treasures. All these lovely things had come from all over the face of the earth to offer her their particular solace. Some had intrinsic beauty of their own. Some had the beauty of association and long use, but all offered comfort to her troubled heart.

Mrs Curdle would pass, as she and her dear husband must pass before long; but the world would go on, as bright and enchanting, and as full of quiet beauty for those that used their eyes to see it, as it had always been.

Mrs Bailey turned off the light, went quietly back to bed and composed herself to sleep.

The houses round Thrush Green now lay in darkness, crouched comfortably against the Cotswold clay like great sleeping cats, their chimneys like pricked ears. Only from two or three of the caravans that huddled together in the centre of the green shone a few small lights from some humble oil lamp or candle flickering there.

Sam and Bella Curdle were thinking of their future. At one end of the caravan lay their three children in heavy slumber, and their parents spoke in low tones.

Sam's last earnings at Curdle's fair stood in a pile on the chair beside their bunk bed. Bella, already in bed, dressed in a shiny pink nightgown of gargantuan proportions, surveyed the money grimly. She had been doing her best to prise from her morose husband his plans for their future livelihood, but without success.

She watched him now, tugging his shirt moodily over his head. His face emerged, battered from the afternoon's fight which had caused his downfall, and sullen with his wife's questionings. She attacked the goaded man again in a shrill whisper.

'Well, tell us, then. What are you going to do when that little lot's gone? See us all starve?'

Sam finished undressing before he spoke. Then he answered her slowly.

'There's a farmer-chap up the Nidden road wants his sugar beet hoeing. I done it afore. We could take the caravan that way and settle there for a bit.'

'How long will that take?' asked Bella stiffly. Her pride quivered at the thought of her husband undertaking such low work. Worse was to follow.

'Three or four weeks. And you could do some too!'

Bella gasped at the shock.

'And what about the kids?' she protested.

'Won't hurt them either,' said her brute of a husband. He turned out the oil lamp and clambered into bed beside her.

'And you'd get some of your fat off,' said Sam savagely, hauling at the bedclothes, and adding insult to injury.

Much affronted, his wife turned her face to the wall. The fumes from the oil lamp crept uncomfortably about the darkness and Bella's misery grew. Two tears of self-pity rolled down to the pillow.

Bella had never liked work.

Ben Curdle heard St Andrew's chimes ring out the half-hour as he was propping a snapshot of Molly above his bed.

He ought to be asleep, he told himself. There was plenty to do in the morning, clearing up the show and setting off on the road again, besides seeing his girl.

So much had happened that he was too excited to think of sleep.

He had accomplished the two tasks he had set himself

that morning as he had rested on Thrush Green's dewy grass. He had found Molly and he had confounded his cousin Sam, the thought of whose mean treachery still made Ben's hot head throb with fury.

But more than that had happened to Ben, the full significance of which he barely realized yet. He looked back to that solemn meeting with his grandmother earlier that evening and marvelled again.

She had returned from her visit to Doctor Bailey with renewed vigour. Ben had not seen her eyes so bright or her bearing so resolute for many a long month. She had closed the door of the caravan, had motioned him to sit, and had taken her own majestic stance upon the red plush stool by the fire. Then she had begun to talk to him as she had never done before.

Out it had all poured. She spoke of his dear father, in words that moved him unaccountably; she spoke of her love for Ben himself, which had touched him so much that he had forgotten all embarrassment, and then she spoke of her own health and disabilities and her need for his help.

She did what Ben had never thought possible. She put into words all that that telling glance had said when they had confronted each other immediately after the fight. She spoke to him, not as one in authority, but as a partner who asked for help and knew that it could be given. Ben was accepted as joint master of the Curdle business and he vowed that he would see it thrive.

The old lady had turned to practical matters. She had shown him her rough and ready ways of calculating expenses, and had given her reasons for following certain routes year after year. She had warned him against certain districts, against unwelcoming councils, and against doubtful members of the Curdle tribe itself.

Ben had listened fascinated. Much he already knew, but much he learnt that night. His happiest moment had been when the old lady praised his Molly and told him that she would welcome her to the family.

But his most triumphant moment had come later, when Mrs Curdle had put a chair beside her own at the card table, and they had sat side by side with the weekly wages arranged before them. The Curdle tribe, awaiting their rewards, had goggled at the sight.

Mrs Curdle had presented Ben to them with much the same air as the monarch presents his prince to the people of Wales.

'Ben,' she said proudly, her hawk gaze raking the assembled company, 'is my partner now. Any orders he gives are to be obeyed, as mine are.'

There was a murmur of assent, for this had been long expected, and young Ben was popular.

'Won't be long,' continued Mrs Curdle, 'before I'm dead and gone. Ben'll carry on for me.'

Ben had gazed modestly at the green baize of the table while his grandmother spoke and had waited for her next remark.

It had come with her habitual tartness.

'Stop gawking and pay out!' she had snapped, nudging him sharply. And Ben, partner and heir, had meekly obeyed.

Now, in the stillness of his own caravan, he tried to realize his overwhelming good fortune, but it was too great to understand.

Dizzy with happiness, he flung his clothes into a corner, took a last look at Molly's photograph, turned out the light, and fell almost immediately into deep sleep.

Only one light glimmered now upon Thrush Green.

Old Mrs Curdle had set her candle on the chair by the bed and its small flame flickered in the draught from the half-door.

The old lady leant upon the sturdy lower half and gazed meditatively at the sleeping world about her.

The skewbald ponies were tethered nearby and she could hear them cropping steadily at the grass. Far away an owl hooted from Lulling Woods and, nearer in a garden, a love-sick cat began its banshee wailing.

The air was still and deliciously warm. Summer had begun with that sunny May day and Mrs Curdle thought of those happy busy months which lay ahead.

Within a few hours her little home would be rumbling along the lanes again between the flowery verges and the quickening hedges.

Her mind roamed ahead visualizing the villages she knew so well, rosy-red brick ones, some with whitewashed walls and grey or golden thatch, and some, like dear Thrush Green, built of enduring Cotswold stone.

Ah, a travelling life was the best one, thought old Mrs Curdle happily. With Ben beside her, and her fears put to rest by her old friend Doctor Bailey, she felt she could face the leisurely jolting miles of summer journeyings. All would be well.

She took a last long look at Thrush Green. The old familiar houses slept peacefully awaiting the dawn. The last light, in the doctor's sitting-room, had gone out and she alone was still awake.

High above her St Andrew's clock chimed midnight, and then the slow notes telling the passing of another day floated upon the night air.

'Twelve,' counted Mrs Curdle, straightening up. 'Time I was abed.'

She closed the top of the door slowly.

'I've never been to Thrush Green yet without feelin' the better for it.'

She climbed heavily into bed, sighing happily.

'Ah, well! I've had a good day,' said Mrs Curdle, and blew out the light.

MORE ABOUT PENGUINS
AND PELICANS

Penguinews, which appears every month, contains details of all the new books issued by Penguins as they are published. From time to time it is supplemented by *Penguins in Print*, which is our complete list of almost 5,000 titles.

A specimen copy of *Penguinews* will be sent to you free on request. Please write to Dept EP, Penguin Books Ltd, Harmondsworth, Middlesex, for your copy.

In the U.S.A.: For a complete list of books available from Penguins in the United States write to Dept CS, Penguin Books, 625 Madison Avenue, New York, New York 10022.

In Canada: For a complete list of books available from Penguins in Canada write to Penguin Books Canada Ltd, 2801 John Street, Markham, Ontario L3R 1B4.

THE HEART OF LONDON

Monica Dickens

The altered expression of post-war London, seen through the eyes of a wealth of entertaining personalities – the residents of Cottingham Park, a typical metropolitan area.

Monica Dickens applies all her sympathy and humour to the day-to-day eddies of a changing society.

Also published

The Angel in the Corner

The Fancy

Flowers on the Grass

The Happy Prisoner

Man Overboard

Mariana

One Pair of Feet

One Pair of Hands

My Turn to Make the Tea

Thursday Afternoons

Winds of Heaven